No Tears for my Father

a true story of incest

by

Viga Boland, B.A.

*****

TRIGGER WARNING:

This is a true story. The graphic descriptions and language could cause flashbacks and discomfort for sensitive readers, especially those who have themselves been victims of incest or childhood sexual abuse. However, *"that's the way it happened and that's how it must be told."*

© 2013 by Viga Boland, BA. The book author retains sole copyright to his or her contributions to this book.

This is a work of non-fiction, a true story of incest. All characters depicted in the story are, or were, real people in the author's life.

First edition published August, 2013

Second edition published November, 2013

Third edition published May, 2015

ISBN: 1512212423 (CreateSpace)

ISBN13: 978-1512212426 (CreateSpace)

Photos ©John Boland.

Poems ©Viga Boland

Song lyrics, *"It's Not Over"*, *"Black & Blue"*

©Andrew Rudd and Victoria Boland. www.andrewvictoria.com

Visit Viga Boland below:

http://www.vigaboland.com

http://www.memoirabilia.ca

http://vigaland.blogspot.com

http://www.youtube.com/vigaland

DEDICATION:

This book, written initially at the insistence and encouragement of my two lovely daughters, Kimberley and Victoria, and my dear husband, John Boland, is dedicated first to them.

Secondly, this book is dedicated to all victims of incest and child sexual abuse. It is my sincerest hope that by baring my soul and revealing my past, others who have suffered sexual abuse at the hands of members of their family, will be encouraged and emboldened to finally come out from under the shame they have carried, usually silently, for years, and begin to speak out from under incest and childhood sexual abuse.

It is my firm belief that only by telling our stories of incest and child sexual abuse can we begin to heal. As well, I hope that by doing so, those currently being abused will refuse to stay silent any longer, because

"Victims' own voices are the best weapons against child sexual abuse."

© *Viga Boland*

"It's easier to deny malevolence than it is to face it"
Dr. Anna Salter

ACKNOWLEDGEMENTS/THANKS:

Telling this story would not have been possible without the love and encouragement of my husband, **John Boland**, and my two beautiful daughters, **Kimberley** and **Victoria**. No words can ever fully express my gratitude for the love they have always given me over the years, even when the demons of my past took me so low that sometimes I couldn't show them just how very much I truly loved them too.

The other person whom I must thank is **Andrew Rudd**. His willingness to help me through the technical maze of setting up this self-published book was amazing. I called on him, interrupting his own work time and again, and nothing was too much to ask of him. Andrew, you're a genius, mate, and I can't thank you enough!

To my dear friend and fellow-author, **Kate Walker**, my deepest appreciation. It was your encouragement and reassurance that I could, and should write that kept me believing that one day, I would indeed get that book out of me. Thanks Kate.

I also want to thank **Colleen Laylon**, **Diane Quinn**, and **Kate** for your feedback on this book before it saw print. Thanks too to author and facilitator, **Martyn Kendrick,** for putting the ink in my pen and getting me started.

I must also thank those members of my private Facebook Group, who, without knowing it, made me more determined daily with each of their posts, to write this true story of incest. Their own pain confirmed the need there is for victims to Speak Out From Under Incest.

Last but not least, thanks to all of you who have supported my work by purchasing a copy of this book. I hope you will tell others about it, especially other victims of incest who must COME OUT FROM UNDER and SPEAK OUT FROM UNDER INCEST. Thanks for reading my story.

COME OUT FROM UNDER

When you finally come out from under
And absolve yourself of blame
When you cast aside the crippling fears
And rid yourself of shame

As you peel away the layers
To expose the soul below
You will come to love that person
The one you didn't know:

The one you lost so long ago

©Viga Boland, 2012

CONTENTS:

INTRODUCTION	7
MY MUSE	8
PART 1: CHILDHOOD	PAGE 9 - 43
PART 2: ADOLESCENCE	PAGE 44 - 114
PART 3: ADULTHOOD	PAGE 115 - 196
AFTERMATH	PAGE 197 - 203
DEAR READER	PAGE 204 - 206
POETRY	PAGE 206 - 214
FACTS ABOUT CHILD SEXUAL ABUSE	PAGE 215 - 216
ABOUT THE AUTHOR	PAGE 217 – 218
BOOK EXCEPRTS	PAGES 219 ff

TODAY: 2013

Admittedly, she's an odd sight. I watch her getting out of the little red 1991 Chevy Sprint at the local Y and it's hard not to laugh.

She's nearly lost inside the oversized, black-hooded parka trimmed with mustard-yellow cotton fleece whose colour matches the words, "Hamilton Swimming" stitched across the back. She looks out of place in the parka: it's something a young member of a swim club would wear. But she's old.

Careful not to slip, she navigates the slushy snow of the Y parking lot. Her large black sports duffle bag, jammed tight with a swimsuit, a huge bath towel, shampoo, face, foot and other creams for super dry skin looks heavy. On the bag, emblazoned again in that same bright mustard colour, are the letters "HWAC". This must have been her child's bag.

She comes to the Y pool two or three times a week for her workout ... a workout that is not just physical. As she counts each stroke of each of the forty laps, with her mind focussed only on her swimming and the beautiful sensation of being embraced by the water, she feels herself being cleansed yet again of the excrement of a past that left a young pre-teen feeling soiled and dirty for years to come.

Now, forty-five years later, the old lady lost inside her daughter's black swimming parka is ready at last to come out from under her hidden past and share her story of incest. The old lady in the black parka is me. And this is my life's story.

My Muse

The voice I hear is that of a teen
Not woman, not child,
but someone between
It is her words that guide my pen
To stop, remember, and write again

Her mind is young in a body old
She tells the story she's never told
Baring the secrets behind her shame
And hoping others will do the same
And

COME OUT FROM UNDER INCEST

©*Viga Boland 2013*

PART 1: CHILDHOOD

CHAPTER 1: DARLINGHURST, AUSTRALIA

When did my life begin? On paper, it was February 13, 1946. But that paper just proves I fought life's first big battle and came out of it alive. No, life for me began with my first memories, and those begin in Australia.

Dipping way back, I see a little girl in a tiny, narrow backyard, surrounded by a super high fence at the back of a dark, skinny row house in Darlinghurst, a suburb of Sydney. Darlinghurst neighbors the notoriously famous King's Cross. It's in this narrow row house which has only two windows, one in front and one in back, that life begins for me.

I lived there 5 days of the week with Mrs. Nastrom. I'm sure she had a first name ... Elsie or Dulcie or something like that ... but to me she was only Mrs. Nastrom. She was gray-haired, somewhat frumpy, but kind. She was always good to me. If she ever yelled at me, I don't remember it. That says a lot about her because it's much easier to remember the bad that people do to us. As Shakespeare wrote in his play, JULIUS CAESAR:

> *"The evil men do lives after them*
> *The good is oft interred with their bones"*

That applies more to my father, but he takes up most of this story and for now, I want to start on a positive note.

Mrs. Nastrom looked after me while my parents worked because where they rented, in Surry Hills, children were welcomed only on weekends. I still don't understand why that was so: my weekend behavior was no different from my weekday behavior. If anything, I was more active and noisy on the weekends!

It's odd, but I have more memories of Mrs. Nastrom and Darlinghurst than of my parents and Surry Hills. Perhaps that's because I enjoyed staying with Mrs. Nastrom more. Even though her living room carpet was full of fleas that jumped all over me when I sat on the floor, I was reasonably happy there: no-one yelled at me.

I can see her living room now. From where I sat with the fleas playing hop-scotch on my legs, I could see her husband's big armchair. Beside it was a tall spittoon ... yes, it's for what you think it's for ... and it was quite disgusting. He would sit in that armchair, reading the paper, and every so often he'd hack up something and expel it into that spittoon. I was amazed he never missed. I'd half wish he would so I would know what he'd do then i.e. would he clean it or would he yell at Mrs. Nastrom to clean it, the way my father would do to my mother, or would it just be left to the fleas? I know that doesn't sound very nice but that is how I thought when I was 4... 5... 6? It's actually rather amazing I even remember thinking like that, given I don't really know how old I was when I started living with the Nastroms. It seemed like a long time but time doesn't exist for most kids.

The other thing I remember in that one-window room was Mrs Nastrom's curio cabinet. It was twice as high as I was and I had to stand on my tippy toes to see all the neat little figurines she had in there. There must have been a hundred or more, everything from miniature dogs, cats and turtles to larger pieces like those blue and white china teapot and teacup sets so common in the 50's. I recall standing and staring at those ornaments for hours hoping Mrs. Nastrom might one day ask me if I'd like to have one, but she never did. She kept that cabinet locked. It was early training for me that life would be full of things I wanted but couldn't have.

The other thing, or rather person, I remember in that house was Mrs. Nastrom's son, Desi. He's probably dead by now too, but he was larger than life for me then. I remember him as being very tall ... but after all, I was very small. He had jet black hair that was slicked back Elvis-style, long before Elvis made that look legendary, and he was always smiling. He had a great set of white teeth. He seemed to flit in and out of that house as frequently as the fleas jumped in and out of the carpet. I'm not even sure if he lived there steadily but I'm pretty sure he had a room upstairs. In all the time I lived there, I never went upstairs ... rather odd considering how naturally curious I was about everything.

I didn't really know much about Desi but I don't remember ever seeing him speak with his father, and the best Mr. Nastrom got from him was a quick peck on the cheek. But he always had a smile for me and he loved tormenting me over who would get the crust on a fresh loaf of bread. Every time he was there for breakfast, he'd call me into the kitchen and ask me:

"Do you want the crispy crust or the nice soft inside slice?"

He must have been in sales as he always seemed to be selling me on the soft inside slice when he knew I really wanted the crunchy crust! He'd taunt me, joking, building my frustration:

"You want the crust, don't you?"

I'd nod, hopeful that crust would be mine this morning.

"We'll I want the crunchy crust too. So what are we going to do about that?"

"You could cut off the other end?" I'd suggest.

That would set him off into fits of laughter before he said Mrs. Nastrom wouldn't like having that lovely fresh bread dry out at both ends. And I would scowl at him as he passed me the soft inside slice and watch him torment me a bit more as he made a show of taking each bite of that crust.

As nice as Desi was, he was busy teaching me just as his mom did that life was full of things I wanted and would really have to work for, and only sometimes would I succeed in getting them. He also was the first male to teach me that I'd also get things I didn't want. My father was the second.

The only other person who dropped in quite often at the Nastroms was the one none of them knew about. Only I knew of her. She had no name and she only ever played with me in that tiny narrow backyard. She never stepped inside the house. She'd suddenly appear out of nowhere, smile at me brightly and ask:

"Want to play pretend princesses?"

When we played pretend princesses, she was the beautiful one and I was the ugly one, a bit like the Cinderella story except there was only the two of us and she was never really mean to me.

"Here," she'd say, "you wear my pretty dress today. There! Don't you look lovely in that!"

And I did feel pretty as I danced around, pretending I was a beautiful ballerina. She would smile and encourage me, telling me I really wasn't that very plain girl I saw in the mirror each morning. That one had mousy brown, straight hair that wouldn't curl; light olive- coloured skin, thankfully minus freckles; a mouth that was always missing a tooth and hazel eyes that couldn't decide if they were green or brown!

When I think about that imaginary friend now, maybe she was really my fairy godmother ... or my guardian angel (I believed in them at that point). I was quite heart-broken when she suddenly stopped visiting. I'd sit on a dirty little wooden stool just beneath that one living room window and wait for what seemed like hours. I'd call her ... it didn't matter that she had no name. I'd squeeze my eyes shut as tight as they'd go wishing her to be there when I opened them. But when she left, she left for good. I never saw her again. Her sudden disappearance enforced my belief I was ugly. Why else would she leave me when I needed a friend so badly? Years later, my father convinced me I was indeed, ugly.

I often wondered why she no longer was there for me, why no-one else ever saw her, what made her leave, and when she actually just disappeared. I think it might have been around the time that I became more acutely aware of the less pleasant sides of life, like the first time I felt real fear.

You see, nice as he was to me, Mr. Nastrom was an alcoholic. Every Friday night he'd be out until after I went to bed. I'd be just falling asleep and I'd hear him come home. He was belligerent. He swore. He cursed Mrs. Nastrom. I'd hear noises, like slapping, then crying and whimpering. I'd lie in my bed, frightened, fearing that Mr. Nastrom would come into my room and hurt me. I'd huddle under my blanket, with one eye open watching the door, trying not to breathe. He'd open the door, look into the room, grunt, then close it again. Everything would be quiet for a moment. Then the cursing and swearing and slapping would start again. I'd fall asleep listening to Mrs. Nastrom sobbing. But it was those Friday nights that started making me fearful of going to bed. I began wetting the bed too. Bed seemed less and less a safe place, and as I would later learn, bed was often anything but safe.

The next morning, I'd notice bruises on Mrs. Nastrom's arms and sometimes on her face but I pretended not to see them. She knew I saw them but her eyes warned me to say nothing. I wouldn't see Mr. Nastrom those mornings as by the time he got up, my parents had arrived to pick me up to take me to the Surry Hills flat for the weekend. I was usually happy to go there after the "Friday night knockdown". I was also already learning to keep my mouth shut about awful things, and as I grew older there were many awful things to keep quiet about.

If my imaginary friend, or fairy godmother, or guardian angel abandoned me at that time, her timing was horrible. That was when I needed her most. That, and the time one of the older girls at my school molested me. She walked home with me one day and invited me to her parent's flat, just down the road close to "the Cross", famous for prostitutes. I was very excited that someone liked me enough to do that. Most people just ignored me.

"Would you like some milk?" She offered. "A biscuit?"

She was so nice to me. I felt very special. I wolfed down the milk and biscuit, hoping she might let me take another one. Suddenly, I desperately needed to go to the washroom. She led me down the hall, but instead of giving me some privacy, she stood there watching as I peed. The toilet roll was empty, so she grabbed a roll from the cupboard, and held onto the empty cardboard roll. As I finished up, she pinned me against the bathroom door, put the empty roll between her body and mine at that private spot, and began moving her own body backward and forward. I had no idea what she was doing or why, but somehow I knew it was wrong.

"Stop! Stop it" I yelled. "What are you doing? Please stop!

I started crying, begging her to let me go home. She got really angry with me but she backed off and pushed me roughly down the hall and out of the flat. I ran back to Mrs. Nastrom's with tears streaming down my face. But when she asked what was wrong, I couldn't tell her. I began to wonder if I'd imagined it all. (That was a process I would repeat many times as I grew up i.e. wondering if I'd imagined what I thought had happened.) I ran into the yard trying to conjure up my imaginary friend. I wanted to tell her what happened.

"Where are you?" I cried. "I need to talk to you. Please, please come visit. I need to tell you something."

But she didn't come. In later years I would learn that when I most needed someone to talk to, there was no-one interested enough in me to listen. And when it came to guardian angels and all those other folks up there who we can turn to in times of need, well, I guess they just weren't there for me either.

The one other memory that sticks out in my mind about my life in Darlinghurst was the local "watering hole", the pub on the corner. Any weekday, but especially on Fridays, the place was full of Aussie men washing away their week in beer. Across the street from that pub was my "stage"...the marble steps of an apartment building and every Friday afternoon you'd see this little girl tap dancing and singing a song for the male audience inside. The men would chat with each other, raise a beer to cheer my poorly executed pirouettes, even clap when I took my bows, and occasionally toss me a penny through the open windows. I'd eagerly run across the street to scoop up my penny, then return to my stage to give them some more of what I believed they genuinely enjoyed.

While I twirled and hummed and sang, I was in another world. I was someone else and I mattered. Someone, even if he was only a drunk, appreciated me. These guzzlers, along with that imaginary friend with whom I played in that narrow garden behind Mrs. Nastrom's row house, were the only ones who understood what was in my heart: a very lonely, only child who desperately needed a friend and some proof that I mattered.

CHAPTER 2: SURRY HILLS

My memories of Surry Hills are really vague beyond the small flat itself that my parents rented. What I can still see quite clearly in the flat is my parent's double bed whose springs squeaked when they thought I was asleep, and my own little cot placed perpendicular to the foot of their bed. Beyond those details of the interior, I recall only the street, Marlborough Street, which ran downhill and on which all the houses were the same: skinny two-storey row houses with wrought iron fences in front of small verandas where no-one sat outside.

The most important thing for me when my parents took me to the Surry Hills flat for the weekend was seeing my first and only real life girl friend, Denise. I wonder if she is still alive today, and if so, does she remember me? Denise was chubby, smiling and always happy. She lived around the corner in a one-storey row house and without fail, she'd come by every Saturday afternoon to see if I could play. Invariably, she'd ask her parents if I could sleep over. They always agreed and my parents breathed a sigh of relief they didn't think I heard when I grabbed my pajamas and left.

But it was the Sunday mornings at Denise's that I loved best. Her dad would make mountains of hot toast dripping with salted butter and Denise and I would dive into that toast, butter running down our chins. We'd laugh and joke with her fat jovial dad (who could have passed for Santa if he were older and had a beard) and who never yelled at us. I'm sure it was at Denise's that I developed a love of hot buttered toast that is still a favorite food to this day. Those hot-buttered-toast Sunday mornings were happy times and I hated going back to the flat to spend the rest of the day with my parents.

The only Sundays I remember enjoying with them are the ones on which we went to Coogee Beach. Oh how I loved that! I'd get so excited as we drove up and down the roller-coaster hill roads leading down to the beach and then suddenly, I'd see it: the beautiful blue waters of an endless ocean sparkling under cloudless sunny skies. My heart would leap into my mouth with joy. I so loved the water. I couldn't get out of the car fast enough and I'd run screaming with excitement into the cooling waves. My father would be yelling at me to stop and wait for him, but the child in me was impatient and sometimes disobedient.

It was on one of these Sunday beach days that I learned the hard way that I should have listened to my father. I remember turning my back on the sea ever so briefly to see where my parents were spreading their blanket, and suddenly the sea picked me up and tossed me over and over and over. I remember my fear, the panic that I was being carried out to sea and would be drowned. Suddenly the sea slammed me hard onto the sand and a huge hand grabbed my arm and dragged me, shocked and gasping for air, out of the waves. My father looked at me with eyes that showed more rage than relief:

"Good thing I saw you, wasn't it? You would have drowned out there!" He was screaming at me. "How many times have I told you not to go into the water without me? How many times! Next time you will be obedient and do what you're told, won't you. Won't you? Answer me!"

"Yes Daddy," I mumbled with eyes downcast.

I never went back into the water that day. I was too scared, not just of the waves but of my father. He had saved me but his fury at my disobedience frightened me more than the ocean.

That night I wet the bed again. It was becoming a regular occurrence. My mother patiently changed the sheets while my father angrily paced back and forth.

"Stupid, disobedient child! How many times have I told you not to wet the bed? How many times!"

Back in a makeshift bed on the floor beside their bed, I slipped into an exhausted but deep sleep. Suddenly I became aware of a loud slurping noise near my face. It got louder and louder and then suddenly "WHACK"! My father's hard, strong hand slapped my mouth, knocking my thumb out of it. He was furious, shouting at me for waking him up with my noisy thumbsucking.

"Bloody child! Big baby! How many times have I told you not to suck that thumb? How many times!"

"Many times Daddy," I sobbed.

My mother was trying to calm him down, reminding him I'd had a big fright that day. But my Father's look was thunderous above my frightened face as he held his hand high, ready to slam me again if I put my thumb back in my mouth, all the while reminding me his belt would be next. I stuck my hand under my back and promised to keep it there till he climbed back into bed. I slept fitfully for the rest of the night, ever terrified of that thumb that seemed magnetically drawn to my mouth and my father's rough hard hand always ready to slap it away and reach for his leather belt.

My fear of going to bed was increasing. Night after night, I'd fall asleep hearing my father's voice asking "How many times?" and my ever repeated answer: "Many times Daddy". Bit by bit, life was giving me more and more reasons to be afraid of the darkness of a bedroom.

On a brighter note, my parents occasionally did pick me up on a Friday night instead of Saturday mornings, and I always liked that for one reason only: Friday night was fish and chip night ... real fish and chips, Aussie style! After picking me up from the Nastroms, Mom and dad would stop at the hot fish and chips shop around the corner from the flat. Oh, how excited I'd get! I can still smell the fish frying, hear the chips sizzling in the fat and feel my pulse quickening with the anticipation of stuffing myself with all that greasy, "bad-for-you" super yummy food. It was even exciting to watch them dump that mountain of sizzling fish and chips onto white paper, fat and all, then ever so quickly wrap it all up in yesterday's newspapers. I thought they were so clever, so skilled in doing this. It was almost artistic. I wanted to be like that one day i.e. so skilled at something that others would be mesmerized by me.

One Saturday afternoon, Denise and I were playing in a parking spot for trucks near a deserted building on the opposite side of Marlborough St. just up a little ways from the flat. It was an Aussie-hot summer afternoon. A man with a camera slung around his neck came along, spotted us, smiled and started chatting with us. We weren't scared of him. We had each other and saw nothing threatening about him. He asked if he could take some pictures of us. We grinned our missing teeth smiles, blushed and agreed. He took a few shots, then asked us to sit together with our backs against the wall. He told us to bring our knees up but to keep them apart.

Our dresses were too short to cover our privates. We tried to pull them over our knees but he said "No... that's great just the way you are." Then he suggested we pull our legs even further apart. I began to feel a little funny about this. Something wasn't quite right. I protested meekly, saying "...but my panties are showing...!" He insisted that was just fine, "Perfect" in fact, just what he wanted. He took several photos. He seemed to be really enjoying what he was doing. I didn't. Neither did Denise, but we had been taught to do what adults told us to. When he was done, he smiled and thanked us and told us he'd give some copies to our parents when he got them developed. That put our minds at ease and we waved goodbye as he continued walking rather quickly up the street. It was only later, much later as I told my parents about him that I realized he never asked who my parents were or where they lived so he could give them the pictures.

My father was always a source of confusion for me: a Dr. Jekyll one day, a Mr. Hyde the next. I remember the day he and I were in a little corner store buying a few basic groceries. My father and the shop owner were having a friendly chat about something. Their voices faded as I lost myself looking at a massive jar of multi-colored loose lollies (Australian for candies). There were hundreds, maybe thousands of lollies in that tall jar. I was fascinated. I reached up with my finger to start counting the lollies. Suddenly the jar slid off the shelf. It crashed to the floor. The lollies spilled everywhere. The shop owner was shouting, angry. My father's face was reddening. I wet my pants, expecting my father's hand to smash into my head any second. I began to cower, but the blow never came. Instead my father was talking quickly, trying to calm down the raging shopkeeper. He was actually blaming the shop owner, suggesting he shouldn't have placed a large glass jar on a slippery glass shelf where anyone could bump it. I could not believe my father was defending me. He'd hit me for far less than this. I was very confused. I did get a walloping however, later at home, when he was telling mom what had happened, and feeling happy that he hadn't been mad at me for breaking the jar, I let my guard down with him and confessed I'd wet my pants. It was another tough lesson in learning to keep my mouth shut around Dr.

Jekyll: the angry Mr. Hyde was never far below the surface of the smiling Dr. Jekyll.

I'm not sure exactly how old I was when my parents told Mrs. Nastrom I wouldn't be staying with her anymore, but I do know it was a shock for both her and me. Her hand went straight to her chest in her loosely buttoned, frumpy blouse and I could see her heart heaving hard beneath it. I ran to her side and buried my head in her long skirt, wrapping it around me in some vain hope my father wouldn't be able to find me there. Tears poured down my face. They told Mrs. Nastrom they'd bought their own home in Yagoona and now I would be living with them as that's how it should be after all.

As they pulled me away from the kindest person I knew, she asked me if I would like to take one of her dolls. These were big dolls she kept in boxes in the front room. She sometimes had let me play with them. Some were big walking dolls that became my friends when my invisible friend left. I talked to them constantly. The others were smaller, the kind you cradle and rock. I sang to those. There was one in that lot that I loved more than all of them. She had a beautiful face but was missing one eye. I always felt so sorry for her. She was so little and already permanently wounded. She and I were one. I clutched her tightly to my aching heart as my father drove me away from a life that was far from perfect but somehow safer and nicer than the life ahead of me. My little doll had only one eye; the adults in my life had two. But that little doll saw my pain and fear and understood me better than any adult ever would.

CHAPTER 3: YAGOONA

Back in the 50's, Yagoona was a sleepy little immigrants' town on the Hume Highway. It was just up the road from Chullora where the immigrants who survived WW2 settled in barrack-style homes, worked hard and hoped a better life would be theirs in this sunburned country. All had the same goal: huddle together, work hard, save, save, save and get that deposit for a home in nearby Yagoona or Bankstown. Mom and Dad were among the first to reach that goal.

Our new home was a brick box with an outhouse way up the back i.e. no inside toilet. That meant climbing out of a warm bed in the absolute dark of the night and making a run to the outhouse hoping the boogie man wouldn't get me and that there were no spiders on the toilet seat. It was so dark in there, no way would I close the door! We couldn't afford toilet paper, so we wiped ourselves with newspaper sheets that dad cut into perfect 12" squares and hung on a hook.

It was in Yagoona that my bed-wetting problem came to a head, maybe because getting up at night to run to the outhouse was just too scary for me, or maybe because I was just a scared child. I can remember being in the deepest sleep, dreaming I needed to go to the toilet, dreaming I got there on time and feeling so much better as I relieved myself thinking my father wouldn't be mad at me this time. I'd feel this lovely warm sensation spreading under my back, up to my shoulders and then suddenly it started to feel cold and wet and I panicked, leaping out of my sleep and off my bed to turn on the light. I'd stand there horrified, looking at the huge wet stain already turning yellow on the sheets, and out of nowhere my father would be beside me, yelling at me, raging, shouting:

"How many times have I told you not to wet the bed? How many times! Look what you've done you stupid girl! Look at the mess you've made. Help your mother get those sheets off the bed! Look at the mattress! Look what you've done. Seven years old and still wetting the bed. What is wrong with you?"

I'd stand there, a sobbing, shaking, frightened mess till my father punched me in the shoulder and told me to get moving. Then they left me to sleep on a blanket on the hard wooden floor while they slipped back beneath the warm blankets in their own room. I'd cry myself back to sleep, vowing to never let it happen again, but it did. Like the thumbsucking, I now had another reason to fear going to bed at night. Over the years, my father would give me many more.

The house in Yagoona was as barren as the outhouse was basic. I remember it vividly: two equal-sized rooms at the front, one a dining room with a glass door to a tiny veranda, the other my parents' bedroom. Behind those, two more bedrooms, one of which was mine. The other was filled with boxes of stuff. Behind those were two more large rooms, one a sunroom, the other the kitchen eating area attached to a small separate cooking area with stove, fridge and sink. The only other room in the house was the bathroom with tub, shower and one sink located between my and my parents' bedrooms.

What sticks out most in my mind about our new home was its barren coldness, the lack of furniture: nothing but the bare necessities...beds, a dressing table in the parents bedroom and table and chairs in each of the dining room (which we never used) and the kitchen. That was it!

No living room couches. No dressers for me. My few bits of clothing were in a couple of boxes in my room. Apart from my one-eyed doll, I had no toys. The only other box in my room held some books. The house was so cold and empty that conversation echoed off the walls and sounded hollow. Home was never warm to me, not then, not later.

There wasn't much food in the kitchen cupboards either. I was often very hungry. Sometimes mom would bring home packets of biscuits from Peek Freans where she worked and that was a big event for me: I'd be allowed to pick one cookie from the lot. No cookies ever took any child as long to eat as that one chosen cookie took me.

I remember my dad picking up mom from Peek Freans on Fridays after work. Those days, I'd be with him. Mom would come out laughing and smiling with the other girls, still wearing her little white uniform and netted cap to keep her hair in. For some reason, her smile would vanish almost as soon as she squeezed into the car's front seat, squishing me between herself and Dad. She smelled so sweet from all the biscuits, I wanted to eat her, but the best I got was a quick kiss on the cheek. She never looked particularly happy to see either dad or me. I had no idea why. I was always happy to see her but I never felt any warmth from her.

Moving to Yagoona meant another huge change for me: school. I was enrolled in St. Felix's Catholic School. My most vivid memory of my first few days there was the marching into class to music piped through loudspeakers. All the kids lined up quickly and neatly as soon as the opening bell sounded and almost immediately the music started up: "1, 2, 3, 4...Whoosh a-whoosh a-whoosh" we all sang as we marched in time, neat rows filing into our classrooms. I remember being embarrassed at not being able to get my feet right i.e. I always started the march on the wrong foot! The other girls would giggle and point at me. I felt super dumb and clumsy in my shiny heavy black shoes, which dad bought for me brand new after telling the salesman I needed shoes with steel toes and soles the way I wore fancy shoes out in no time. So I wore heavy boy's Oxfords while all the other girls wore dainty Mary Janes. I couldn't understand why other girls weren't as hard on shoes as dad said I was. Why was I so different from the rest? To use the modern vernacular, I felt like such a geek.

It was in Yagoona that I had my first remembered encounter with sexual molestation by a man and also my first experience of death. The man was the father of a classmate. The death was that of a kitten. The two events are connected only by the time frame in which they occurred.

Feeling lonely one afternoon after school when I had no homework, I decided to drop by my classmate's house. To my disappointment, she and her sister had gone to the shop for something. Their dad, a very friendly, nice man whom I'd met several times before when I played with the girls, invited me to come in and wait for them.

"They should be here in about twenty minutes," he said. "Why don't you come in and cool off under the fan. It's so hot today!" He wiped the perspiration off his brow.

"Would you like a nice cold lemonade?" he asked as I stepped inside the darkened living room.

"Yes please!" I responded eagerly. This was a nice dad. I wasn't afraid of him as I was of my own father.

He brought me the lemonade and some biscuits and patted the spot beside him on the couch.

"Here, come sit down beside me and tell me about your day at school."

Without hesitation, I plunked myself happily beside him and sipped my lemonade, answering his questions between mouthfuls of the biscuits. I felt very much at home. When he suggested I sit on his lap while he read me a story, I jumped up eagerly and nestled into his arms. As he read, I was so absorbed in the story I didn't notice at first that his hand not holding the book, was caressing my upper thigh. Then suddenly, that hand had slipped inside my panties near that most private place and was probing ever so delicately around. I flushed and shifted, squeezing my thighs together, wanting him to withdraw his hand. No-one ever touched me there, not even my mother.

"What...what are you doing?" I asked, a little scared now, no longer comfortable with my classmate's dad.

"It's okay," he said soothingly. "I do this with Amy

and Sarah all the time when I'm reading to them. It's nothing, just something daddies do to their little girls. They don't mind it at all."

"Well, my Daddy doesn't do it to me," I replied with uncertainty. "Should I tell him you do it to your daughters and ask him to do it to me too?"

"Oh no!" he replied quickly. "Don't do that! Leave it to him to decide when it's time for that. For now, just keep it a secret between you and me okay? Here...here's a ten-pence for you to buy some lollies."

He handed me a ten-pence piece and I hopped off his lap. "I don't know what's taking the girls so long," he said.

"You're welcome to wait if you want?"

All I wanted was to get away from him. No matter what he said, it didn't feel right. It felt like that time the girl in Kings Cross had molested me in the bathroom. I felt ashamed. I didn't know what either of them had done or wanted or why I felt ashamed, but I did, and all I wanted to do was get away from him.

"No ... thanks ... no, I have to go now. It's getting late. Thanks for the lemonade and biscuits."

As I bolted for the door, he said, "If you come visit again and let me read to you, I'll give you a whole shilling. Would you like that?"

I didn't answer him. I slammed the screen door and began running. I could see Amy and Sarah in the distance. They waved and I waved back but no way was I going back to their house, not this time, not ever!

Upset, and starting to cry, and still not knowing why I felt so bad, I wandered through some houses under construction at the end of our street. It was there that I came across a bundle of tiny kittens mewing hungrily behind some rubble. I picked up the smallest one. Its eyes were barely open and it wasn't making a sound. It was so wee and lovely and I wanted it so badly, but there was no-one to ask if I could have it, so I just took it anyway. Its tiny little bony body felt warm and somehow comforted and soothed me after my upset. I carried it home, talking to it, telling it not to be afraid, that I would look after it forever.

I have no recollection whatsoever how my parents reacted to it, or if I even showed it to them. (I was learning to sneak around: honesty only brought beatings.) I remember desperately trying to feed the tiny kitten some milk in a saucer.

"Come, little kitty," I'd whisper to it lovingly. "Please have a sip. You must eat. You must!"

The kitten didn't touch it. So I put some milk on my finger and tried to force the milk into its tiny mouth. When it wouldn't eat, I cupped its tiny furry body in my hands, and hugged it to my chest. I could feel its fragile ribs sticking out as I willed it to somehow take some strength and nourishment from me.

Two days later, I came home from school to find it dead. My heart broke. I lifted up its now cold, already stiffening body and rubbed the fur hoping to restore some warmth into that tiny lifeless body. Tears poured down my face as I absorbed the reality: my beloved kitten was dead and wouldn't be coming back to life. I buried it in the park behind our house, and for the next week, I dug it up every day after school, refusing to believe it was truly gone. Why did life give you things only to take them away before you were ready to let them go?

My dead kitten taught me how hard it is to hold onto things you love. I'd lost my imaginary friend; I'd lost Mrs. Nastrom. And now I'd lost my tiny kitten. What was it about me that life kept taking away what I loved?

CHAPTER 4: WAGGING SCHOOL

But life wasn't always bad. It's just that too often when I thought things were good, they turned bad, like the one and only time I "wagged school". That's Australian for playing hookey. I'm not sure how old I was: seven? Maybe eight already? I guess the devil was speaking to me a little louder than that angel who, according to the school nuns, sat on my other shoulder, but I just decided I wasn't going to school that day. It's not that I didn't like school. I did like it. I think playing hookey was more about me wanting to have some control over my actions, my life. My father was so strict and so controlling all the time. Somewhere inside me rebellion was slowly growing. So that day I decided to rebel and it was fun ... at least at first.

Mom and dad left for work very early every morning. I had to get myself ready for school and walk myself there: none of this driving kids to school or being put on buses by parents or guardians like we have today. Today mom and dad would have been reported to Children's Aid. Well this particular day I decided it'd be more fun to loaf around the house with no parents telling me what to do every minute. I could read, nap, play with my few toys and daydream. The only downside was not being able to go outside for fear the "nana" next door might spot me and tell my parents. Of course, by the time school would have finished, I was getting bored and couldn't wait for Marie, nana's grandchild, to get home. I was bored but feeling great about being so naughty, so enamored with being my own boss, that I couldn't wait to tell her about my day. I swore her to secrecy.

"It was great! I lay around in bed, read a book, played, drew pictures...and no parents or teachers telling me what to do! "

"But weren't you scared being all alone?" Marie asked. She was a tiny, nervous little thing. "What if you hurt yourself or something?"

"Well then, I'd run to your nana's!" I replied with bravado.

"Yes, but then she'd wonder why you were home alone in the first place!"

Marie may have been tiny and nervous, but she wasn't stupid. I hadn't thought of that possibility. My mind had been focused on feeling free. I dismissed her question, but then feeling really daring, I talked her into wagging school with me the next day. And wag we did...until she got scared and bored and wanted to go home early. And of course, nana put two and two together and my gig was up!

Well didn't all hell break loose when nana told my father what I'd done. My dad's face reddened with anger, and he told nana to stick around to see how he dealt with a naughty child. All eyes were on him as he undid his leather belt, pulled it through the trouser loops and turned to me where I was seated on one of the hard kitchen chairs.

"Stand up!" he demanded sternly.

I scrambled off the chair, my eyes downcast, feeling my stomach lurch. I knew what was coming next: it was nothing new to me.

"Lean over the chair on your tummy," he shouted. I did as I was told.

"Pull your pants down!" he demanded. I hesitated, starting to cry, more from shame at having Marie and her Nana see my bare bum than from fear of the beating I knew was coming.

"Did you hear me?" he yelled. "Pull your pants down and stop crying. Now!"

I pulled my pants down and waited for the first lash of that belt, trying not to cry, sniffling and hoping there wouldn't be too many lashes. Whoosh! Down it came, stinging me with its ferocity. I jerked and screamed in pain, my shame forgotten.

"Don't scream!" he yelled as he brought it down again and again. I burst into tears. I heard mama yell, "Bogdan! Stop!" But he didn't. Two more lashes and Nana and Marie started toward the door, almost running through the screen in their rush to get away. One more lash and his anger was spent. I was sobbing uncontrollably. Mama was crying with me.

"Get up!" he commanded, as he threaded the dreaded belt back through the pant loops. "Come over here. Now! MARCH!"

Struggling to pull my pants back up over my burning backside, I stumbled over to him as fast as I could and stood in front of him, too terrified to look at him.

"Look at me!" he demanded. "So how do you feel now? Was your day off school worth it?"

He began laughing, taunting me almost, enjoying watching me squirm. He turned to mama. "Next time, it'll be worse!" he promised us both.

Needless to say, there was no more wagging school, but unfortunately there were many more next times for other infractions, and each time, the punishments became more brutal, regardless of how big or small the offense. My fear of him grew with every event. I became terrified of angering him: it took so little to set him off.

One time he exploded simply because I couldn't pronounce the word "indignantly". I had been doing my reading homework and asked him what the word was. He told me to sound it out, pronounce it. I tried and tried but couldn't spit it out correctly. I saw his face begin to twitch with anger as he made me pronounce it over and over again. As my fear increased, my mind went completely blank, as it would many more times in the years ahead when I was afraid of him. I'd simply freeze, zone out and hear nothing. All I could think of was the impending thump on my head or back, or slam into my ears. My zoning out infuriated him. His rage spilled over and he grabbed my head and smashed my nose again and again into the hard wood of the kitchen table.

"You stupid, stupid, disobedient child!" He screamed at me. "Why don't you listen? How many times do I have to tell you how to say it? How many times! IN-DIG-NANT-LY! Say it! Say it!" And he slammed my face into the hard wooden table again.

"Ingliglantly," I sobbed. He slammed my face into the table yet again. He looked at my mother who stood by helplessly saying nothing. "See what a stupid moron you gave birth to? Stupid! Stubborn. Just like you! She won't listen!"

Eventually, I got it right and he let me go just in time to run to that outhouse before I wet my pants again. I sat there sobbing and peeing and half wishing I could just fall through the hole and vanish in the stinking pit below. It seemed preferable to going back inside that cold house called home.

One day, my Father came home and called mama and me into the kitchen to show us his new punishment toy. He told us it would be used in place of the leather belt if needed. He then proudly produced an authentic horse whip, whipping it back and forth through the air quickly to demonstrate its potential. The whipping sound was terrifying. I could almost feel it lashing into my buttocks. And to make sure I got the message, he finished his demonstration with a warning:

"Don't ever give me a reason to use this on you. It will tear the skin off your naughty bottom!"

It was a warning I took to heart, praying I'd never make him that mad, and promising myself to always do what he asked when he asked. It was a promise that determined all my future behavior when it came to my father's demands, a promise to myself that I'd live to regret.

I was never allowed to play with Marie after wagging school. With no other children my age on the street, I spent the next couple of years very much alone. I'd come home from school, force myself to do homework before my parents arrived (all hell would break loose if I didn't) and developed a habit of huddling in a side door alcove that faced Marie's home. Sometimes I'd catch a glimpse of her peeking through her curtains. I'd smile and wave but she'd quickly duck away from view. So I just huddled there, drawing pictures, singing to myself or daydreaming.

My daydreams were always the same: I was on a stage wearing a massive hooped crinolined gown. I was very beautiful with long flowing hair. And I was singing! I was Luisa Rainier, who played the magnificent soprano in the movie, "The Great Waltz" standing up in the carriage and thrilling all who watched and listened with "The Voices of Spring". Or, other times, I was Dorothy Dandridge in "Carmen Jones", teasing all the men with my tight skirt and low-cut blouse as I warbled out "There is a cafe on the corner ."

My parents loved going to the movies, especially musicals, and had taken me to see both of these more than once. I was enthralled by the stories, the beauty of the actresses and the sound of their voices. And more than anything, I wanted to be them. How ironic I should choose two such contrasting heroines: as time went on, and thanks to my father, except for being beautiful, I evolved into both of them, but not in the way I wanted to, or ever dreamed I would.

CHAPTER 5: Dr. JEKYLL and Mr. HYDE

The Dr. Jekyll and Mr. Hyde personality of my father all through my childhood, into my teens, adulthood and even now in my old age has always puzzled me. How could he be so kind, loving and caring for me one minute, and a raging monster the next, and so often with little or no provocation?

Just to clarify my confusion, let me share two more instances from my childhood that stand out in my memories.

The first involved my mom. She wasn't a happy woman when she was around Dad, and I never felt she had much use for me either ... more like she was my mother in name only. Given what I learned of their relationship when I was much older, I understand that now: as a young refugee during WW2, who was torn away from her family by the Germans in the middle of the night and taken at 14 to work in the labor camps, her adolescence was no happier than mine, but for different reasons.

She met dad in the camp when she was 16. He fell madly in love with her but she never loved him. It was wartime and she had no-one, so he looked after her. One night in the trenches as the planes still patrolled overhead just after the war ended, I was conceived. So there she was, 17 and pregnant to a man she didn't love. Whatever pressures they were under, it didn't take long for Dad's violent nature to surface after they got married. I remember her telling me many years later how he kicked her off the bed and onto the floor, then continued to kick her in her swollen belly because of something she said that upset him. Another time he forced her down on her knees, demanding she kiss his little finger to acknowledge his dominance over her. She refused. The beating that followed her "disobedience" convinced her once and for all that opposing him was futile. She turned into a quiet little mouse who went to work, cooked his meals, cleaned the house and had little time for me, who after all, had come along, unwanted, and unfortunately for us both, chained her to him forever. No wonder I felt she had an unspoken resentment of me all my life.

So this first occasion I alluded to earlier, occurred after dinner one evening. They were both sitting at either end of that kitchen table reading the paper. Mom hadn't said a word to me since she'd come home from work. She looked tired and fed up with everything. Feeling sorry for her and needing some mothering myself, I went over to her and put my arms around her, forcing my face between her and the paper. Suddenly, like a startled horse, she flung a wet dishrag still in her hands from doing the dishes hard across my face. I jumped, not from pain but from shock and immediately started to cry. My dad, to my surprise, yelled at my mom:

"What's the matter with you! What did you do that for?" He looked super angry. He came over to me and put his arms around my shoulders consolingly. He continued to yell at her: "What kind of mother are you? She just wanted to hug you!"

My mother didn't reply. She just went back to the paper and didn't speak to either of us for the rest of the evening. She never did apologize and I never got that hug from her that I needed. On the other hand, I think she's the one who needed the hug but it would be many more years and we were both getting old before we learned to console and hug each other like mother and daughter.

The other time my father did his Jekyll and Hyde routine really frightened me, a clear indication of how he took pleasure in another's pain. I had gone swimming at the Bankstown pool, but typical kid, somehow I'd managed to leave my brand new pair of sandals under a bench in my rush to not keep him waiting when he came to pick me up. He was always horribly impatient. We had just pulled into the drive when he asked why I was barefoot. My face flushed as I remembered where my sandals were. Panic rising in me, I blurted:

" I ... I left my shoes at the pool... "

He thumped the steering wheel with his fist. "Which shoes?" he demanded.

"My ...my ... new ...sandals!" I cried, bracing myself for a slap across the head.

Instead, he yelled: "Get out! Get out now and start walking. Get back to that pool and find your shoes. Get out! Get before I hit you, you stupid cow!"

33

I stumbled out of the car and began running. It was a long way to the pool on foot, a good twenty minutes. Tears of fear streamed down my face as I was terrified the pool might already have closed for the day, or worse yet, that someone had taken the new sandals. He would be furious if the latter happened. I ran and ran. It was getting dark. Suddenly, he was there beside me. He'd caught up walking. I guess he'd thought better of me being alone on darkening streets. He smiled, obviously over his initial anger and I began to calm down. Slightly out of breath, I stammered:

"Thank you Daddy... I...was getting a little scared of the dark."

"Yes, I thought you might," he said almost kindly. "You know daddy always looks after you. I wouldn't want something to happen to you."

I began to relax, comforted by his words and presence. He reached into his pocket then and pulled out a small package wrapped in foil.

"Would you like a lolly?" He offered me the candy.

I was pretty hungry after a day of swimming. "Oh, yes please!" I smiled happily at him. He was being so nice to me. I quickly unwrapped the foil and popped the candy into my mouth. It was soft...and tasted awful! I nearly gagged. I couldn't swallow it. I looked at him, my face twisting in revulsion at the taste. He was watching me intently.

"What's the matter?" he asked, a strange smile on his face.

"It tastes horrible! Can I please spit it out?"

"No! Eat it! We don't waste food! Eat it...now!" he commanded.

I closed my eyes and swallowed the horrible thing. I was crying again.

"What...what kind of lolly was that?" I stammered. "It was awful."

He grinned. It was a rather malicious grin, one I'd see too many times over the years ahead. Very calmly, he said:

"It was poison."

I jerked at the thought. Poison? My father had given me poison? My stomach started churning. I wanted to throw up. I looked at him in disbelief. "Poison? You gave me poison, Daddy?" I began crying even harder.

"Yes," he confirmed calmly. "Is it working yet? Are you feeling like being sick? Do you want to throw up? That's the poison working."

He smiled all the while he was speaking. He continued. "You should feel very ill in about 10 minutes, but I will save you."

"How...how?" I asked, feeling weaker with each step.

"I will save you now just by thinking it. There. I've done it. You now will not die from poison. See, you feel better already, don't you? Your daddy can do magic!" he scoffed, smiling again. Then he winked and started laughing.

"You silly girl! Did you really think I would give you poison? What kind of father would I be? It was just yeast. That's why it tasted so bad. Mama asked me to pick some up for her. I was just playing a trick on you, and you believed it. I always tell you that you are stupid. You must be stupid to think daddy would poison you!"

He couldn't stop laughing. I couldn't stop sniffling. We found the sandals under a bench and returned home. By the time we got back, it was dark and mama had dinner on the table. He began scorfing down his food and between mouthfuls, he told mom about the joke he had played on me. He thought it was hilarious. He said she should have seen the look on my face when he told me it was "poison". Mama didn't seem to see what was so funny. Neither did I. I picked at my food, my appetite somehow gone despite my previous hunger.

If I'd had a crystal ball, I would have seen the whole incident as an omen: fathers can, and do poison their daughters.

CHAPTER 6: GET TOUGH

Any other memories of my life in Yagoona are few, scattered and far between. I was allowed to go to the Saturday movie matinee in Yagoona about once a month. I loved that freedom and felt rather grown up going on my own. I had no friends to go with so I learned to like solitude and still do. I also recall being constantly hungry: I was growing quickly but there never seemed to be enough food in the house. Our cupboards were always bare. My parents had very good friends in a neighboring suburb and visited them just about every Friday night. We'd all go to see a musical film together if one was playing, then return to their place for some tea, bread, Polish ham, kielbasa and tomatoes prepared by the grandmother (babchu) in their family. I would devour the food ravenously. The babchu would always ask my parents: "Don't you ever feed her? She eats all the food!" She'd look at me angrily and my father would tell me to leave the kitchen before I'd had my fill. Many years later, on a return trip to Australia as an adult, I visited that family and to my surprise they commented how neglected and hungry I had been as a child. How odd that I didn't realize that for myself.

I do remember being envious of their daughter, Beata, who has stayed in touch all these years despite the miles between us. Beata always had beautiful clothes, wore those lovely Mary Jane shoes all the other kids wore and carried pretty little purses. I had none of these things. My dresses were hand-me-downs or something mom found at thrift shops, and as I mentioned before, my shoes were those heavy, clunky Oxfords that I outgrew faster than I outwore them. As for a purse? Not a chance. As this person told me, my parents always seemed to have enough money to go to weekly movies but never enough to feed or clothe me nicely. I just thought my situation was the usual and Beata's was the exception.

One other recollection I have of Yagoona is that it was there I learned not to cry when I was hurt: my father wouldn't allow it. He believed in "being tough" and he was always saying I was "too soft", "always crying for no good reason".

He drove this point home on a couple of occasions when I had accidents on my bicycle. I'd always been a rather clumsy child, tripping over my feet in those oversized shoes my father bought a couple of sizes bigger so they'd last longer. And when it came to riding my bike, well, on one occasion, those big shoes got in the way. Over I went, hitting the gravel road hard with my feet caught up in the spokes. My knee was on fire with a gravel burn and blood was oozing. I started to cry but something made me look up at our living room window. My father was there, watching me. There was no sympathy nor concern on his face. He simply shook his index finger at me in warning not to cry. I snuffled back the tears, picked up my bike and went into the house to get a band-aid. He was waiting.

"Being clumsy again, eh?" he said as I walked in the back door. "There better not be any damage to that bike... "

"No," I mumbled. "Just my knee... "

Holding back my sobs, I looked up at him, hoping for some consolation. All I got was:

"Well, it's good you didn't cry. You were about to cry, weren't you? But you saw me watching you through the window, didn't you?"

"Yes, daddy."

"Well, good! That's the idea. You're learning to toughen up. Now go get your mother to put a band-aid on it."

The other time, I somehow managed to drive my bike into a very thorny rosebush down a lane. By the time I'd pulled the bike out of the bush, I was absolutely covered in long, bleeding scratches up both arms and legs. I was stinging all over and pushed the bike home, ready to burst into tears the minute I stepped into the house. My father was there. He took one look at me and sternly asked:

"What happened this time!"

"I accidentally steered my bike into that rose bush at the end of the lane," I replied, trying to choke back the tears.

"Don't start crying!" he shouted at me. "Be tough! Don't cry for every little thing that happens to you. Anyway, what were you doing riding your bike down that lane in the first place? How many times have I told you not to ride that bike in the lane? How many times!"

"Many times Daddy ... "

"Well serves you right. That's what you get for disobedience!"

And so it always went. There was never any excuse for tears, not then and not later. Any crying I needed to do had to be done where no-one, especially my father, could see it. I didn't always succeed in holding back the tears, but as the years went on, I did, indeed, at least on the surface, "toughen up!

CHAPTER 7: CANADA CALLING

I was around eleven when my parents announced we'd be moving to Canada. I don't think I was shocked as they had been talking with a friend about moving to a cooler country with mountains and snow for several months prior. It all sounded rather exciting. The friend dared them to do it. He said he wanted to go too, but was married to an Aussie woman who would never allow it. I don't think anyone believed my parents would bite the bullet, but my dad loved the idea of getting back to a more Poland-like climate. My mother never had any say in anything anyway, and as for me, my thoughts didn't count. All I knew was Canada was closer to the big, bad but exciting America where all the movie stars lived and everyone was rich and children weren't hungry. That worked for me.

The night before we flew out, we stayed with that friend and his Aussie wife in Sydney. He kept begging mom and dad not to go ... a bit late for that given he had been the one who first planted the whole idea in Dad's head! What strange creatures adults were!

My parents put me to bed early. I was full of anticipation and my tummy was tied in knots, almost too excited to fall asleep. I dozed off but suddenly bolted upright and vomited all over the bed. The vomit kept coming in violent spasms. Mama rushed into the room with the Aussie lady on her heels. My father stormed into the room looking furious. He swore and cursed me as the women rushed to clean me up and change the bedding.

"Stupid bloody child!" he yelled over and over again. "Just like her to do something like this now! He cursed me again and raised his huge arm to hit me. The Aussie woman stepped between us.

"Stop it!" she yelled at him. "She can't help it! What do you think...that she did this on purpose? Maybe she has a virus or something..."

My father wouldn't be placated. "She'd better not have a bloody virus or I'll give her something to vomit about. She can make us all sick and we're flying in the morning. No, she was just a little pig eating too much again! Get back to bed you little pig and stop vomiting!" He seemed to think I could control the spasms, that I was doing this purpose.

The Aussie lady brought me a cup of sweet black tea. My mother held it to my mouth, encouraging me to drink. I had just swallowed the last mouthful, when before she could take the cup away, the whole cup came right back up straight back into the cup. Despite my upset and tears, I thought it was quite remarkable, even funny. So did the two women. My father just glared at me with threatening eyes. He left the room saying:

"If we have to cancel this trip because of her, she's going to get it! Bad blood! Such a bad child! Always doing something she shouldn't. Always in the way! So stupid!"

I fell asleep terrified I might vomit again, terrified of what would happen to me if they had to cancel the trip and just terrified of being my father's daughter.

I have vague memories of leaving Australia in 1957; I remember seeing a handful of our family friends waving goodbye as I peered through the tiny porthole-like windows of the monstrous (to me) Qantas Super Constellation 88; I had no real understanding of just how far away Canada was from Australia but I expected to see them all again soon. The interior of the plane was cramped and so noisy from the droning engines that we had to yell to each other to speak. We landed on the Phoenix Islands to refuel at midnight. I was unprepared for the clammy humidity of the night air as we disembarked for a short time. My face wrinkled in revulsion at the first sip of the tart island fresh-squeezed juice a pretty lady with dark hair handed us.

I fell back to sleep on the plane and awoke to brilliant sunshine streaming through that tiny plane window. We were landing in Hawaii. Would I see the hula girls our Australian friend had mentioned? There ... there was one! As we disembarked, the beautiful hula girl put a lei over our heads and dropped it gently around our necks. She gave me a quick welcome "aloha" kiss on the cheek. My eyes were big as saucers as I took in the palm trees swaying everywhere to the sounds of melodious Hawaiian music. I thought this must be what heaven was like: a true paradise of smiling happy faces, no anger, only friendliness. I decided if Canada was like this, I'd love it. Maybe all my parents needed to be nice to me was a happier country?

Hours later my father frightened me as we lifted off from San Francisco: he told me that this was where most planes crashed if they didn't get high enough, fast enough to clear the massive mountains. I was petrified, convinced this was the end. I'd never see Canada. Miraculously we made it over the mountain range. I started breathing again and un-gripped my hands from the seat arms. My Father told me I didn't need to worry: he was protecting me over those mountains. I believed him. After all, fathers always protected their children, didn't they?

At last, we landed in Vancouver. My first look at Canada was depressing: it was overcast with light drizzle, humid, dingy-looking. As the taxi took us to a hotel, I stared at the unfamiliar, drab two-storey wooden homes that lined the streets like soldiers all wearing the same uniforms. There were no palm trees, no sunshine. Where were the mountains, those rockies my father had always talked about? I decided I didn't like Canada. It was ugly. So much for thinking we might be a happier family here.

That first night in a Vancouver hotel and for several nights after, sleeping was fitful and fretful. Jetlag. We walked ourselves weary during the day, taking in the bleakness of our surroundings, looking for a furnished rental flat we could move into quickly. But at night, sleep eluded us.

On the second or third night, I became aware of my parents talking in whispers. Naturally curious, I strained to listen. My father's voice grew louder. He sounded annoyed. He was trying to get my mother to do something she didn't want to. Her voice became whiny, complaining. His became louder and more insistent. She went silent. Their bed springs started creaking, almost rhythmically. Another sound emerged and I didn't like it. It sounded sloshy, repulsive for some reason. I tried to cover my ears with my hands. I pulled the pillow over my head. It didn't help. Now my father was breathing heavily, grunting, using dirty words in time to the rhythmic creaking of the springs. My mother was silent. I could barely breathe. I was so scared he'd realize I was hearing all this though I had no idea what it was. Somehow I knew it was that special something only grown-ups do when they think the kids are asleep. I tried again not to listen but suddenly my father let out a big, ugly yell. I jumped thinking he knew I had heard all this and would come over and belt me for listening. But he didn't. When their bed stopped creaking a few seconds later, disturbed and revolted by what I'd heard, I slipped back into a fitful sleep full of ugly, sloshy noises and foul language I didn't understand.

The next morning we went shopping for some food. For some inexplicable reason, I couldn't bring myself to look at my mother's face. I kept looking at her legs, slim and nicely shaped in her high-heeled platform shoes. I took in her pretty flower print dress, noticing the curviness of her hips, the pointiness of her breasts. I looked at her in a way I never had before. I couldn't stop staring at her body, wondering if what he had done with her in bed had to do with her body, and if so, what part of it.

For some reason I couldn't fathom, I suddenly didn't like her. She repulsed me. She looked cheap, but why? Something about her seemed dirty, but what was it? To this day, I don't understand my reaction to my mother on that morning after, but I do remember it truly unsettled me. I think I was disappointed in her for giving in to dad, for letting him get his way when she didn't want to do whatever it was he wanted. Little did I know that within a couple of years it would be me giving in to him, and it would be my body from which the revolting noises would come.

We only lasted a month in Vancouver. My father couldn't find any work so he packed up the only possessions he had...Mom and me... and away we went, this time by train. It was the best way to see Canada he said but the only part that looked nice to me were those Rockies so far in the distance I could barely see them. It would be another 20 years or so before I ever saw them again.

Toronto turned out to be a bit more exciting for all of us as my parents contacted friends whom they had made in the war camps. These were the ones who had chosen Canada over Australia when the refugees were given a choice of countries after the war. Just about none of them had returned to the devastation that was Poland. Canada and Australia were lands of promise and freedom. There was nothing to return to anyway.

For a brief time, one of these families gave us a large room in their High Park home to help us out while dad and mom looked for work. Because of his experience as a tool and dye maker in Australia, he landed a job rather quickly with Massey Harris, later known as Massey Ferguson. With the help of a friend, mom got into Christies Biscuits on the Lakeshore. Both worked for these companies until retirement many, many years later.

The pay was excellent as were the benefits and each eventually had several weeks vacation time. We moved from the friends' home to a small attic apartment on beautiful High Park Blvd, and the world outside my rooftop window looked like a very nice place. Maybe Canada wasn't so bad after all.

PART 2: ADOLESENCE

CHAPTER 8. NOT QUITE RIGHT

The first time I knew something wasn't quite right with my new world was when I was around twelve. We were still renting the attic in that huge older home on High Park Blvd. I loved the area with its tree-lined streets and proximity to everything one wanted, but I came to hate my life there because that's where it all started.

Mom was in the tiny alcoved attic kitchen frying my favorite breaded pork chops for dinner. I was starving and the delicious smell had me salivating. I was on my way to check out her progress and as I passed their bedroom, dad called me inside. He was propped up against pillows relaxing and reading the paper after a day of work at Massey Harris. He beckoned me to his bedside, grinned at me in an odd way, and asked how my school day had gone. As I replied, he poked his head to see around me where I was standing near his bed, looking to see if mom was there I guess. Then he commanded me to come closer to his bed. I obliged, thinking he wanted to share a secret with me.

Well he did, but not quite the secret I expected. In an instant, his hand was up my leg and into that most private spot. I recoiled and jumped back in fright and confusion. Instantly, his fingers went to his lips making a "Shhh..." gesture as he again looked around me to make sure mom wasn't there. He smiled and winked at me reassuringly, and in a soothing voice said:

"Don't be scared, kitten. Daddy was just checking to see if you're developing and growing okay down there ... if everything's forming properly."

His reply made me uneasy. Somehow I didn't believe him but then I couldn't understand why else he would have done what he did. I wanted to believe him. After all, hadn't he told me when he pulled the yeast trick that he was magic? And hadn't he re-assured me in the plane that he was protecting me over those San Francisco mountains? And wasn't it he who jumped to my defense when my mom lost it with that rag across my face? Yes, he was my father and fathers do look out for their children.

"So..." I asked in a small, faltering voice, "is everything okay?"

45

"Everything seems just fine," he whispered "but don't tell your mom about it."

"Why not?"

"Well, you know how your mother is. She might start worrying if she thinks something's wrong that I have to check you out and you don't want mom to worry now, do you? Everything's fine. Now off you go. Ask mama when dinner will be ready. Tell her daddy's starving!"

It's strange how a child instinctively knows when an adult isn't quite coming clean. Though I was totally naive about sex, somehow I knew what daddy had done wasn't right. It wasn't about checking to see if I was developing properly. He had made me uncomfortable. And his explanation about why I shouldn't tell my mother didn't make a lot of sense to me either. But, as he said, I didn't want to worry her, so I worried myself instead. He never "checked up on my development" again. The next time, he approached me more directly, removing any doubts in my mind that something wasn't quite right behind the closed doors of our home.

Apart from that first lesson, my recollection of life in the attic is very skimpy except for a few things. I remember spending afternoons after school peering through my high attic bedroom window watching for daddy to come home from work and wishing he wouldn't. I remember that's where I had my first period and was terrified I would bleed to death before mama got home to save me and explain what was happening to me. No-one had prepared me for this! I remember her stuffing cotton wool in me and in my underwear, then rushing up the street with me to the corner drugstore where she bought me a box of Kotex napkins and the pharmacist gave me a free booklet on "all you need to know about menstruation." And I remember my terror at the knowledge that I could now get pregnant. But I consoled myself with the thought that that could only happen if I had sex...and I planned to stay a virgin forever.

The other thing I remember most about the attic was our living room. We had an old bed chesterfield and a small

T.V. When dad came home from work, the first thing he did was open up the bed of the chesterfield and lie down on it. When dinner was ready, the three of us would recline on the chesterfield, holding our plates in our laps as we had no table at which to sit. After dinner, mom would start to nod off and dad would consistently suggest she go take a nap in their bedroom. She always took his suggestion. Once she was gone, dad would pull back a blanket and tell me to come cuddle with him. I didn't want to but I knew that opposing him would make him angry. So I did as I was told. Little did I know that this evening procedure in our attic would become the pattern of my life for the next eleven or so years and would permanently change any plans I had of remaining a virgin.

When my father gave me my first lesson in sex ed, or rather, incest ed, we no longer lived in the attic. We were now renting a very large ground floor flat just around the corner. It was there that my father violated my body, stole my adolescence, turned me into his punching and kicking bag, and taught me my life would never be fully my own.

Lesson #1, learning how powerless a woman can be with a man on top of her, took place on a school day, as did most of my lessons. It was my bad luck mom left for work long before I got up and my father also had to leave. I had just come awake and was stretching, anticipating the day ahead, when suddenly my father appeared in the doorway to my room. He completely startled me. I swallowed hard and felt a knot growing inside my stomach. My palms started to sweat. He was standing there in only his underwear: singlet and briefs.

As he started over to my bed, I drew the blankets up tightly around my neck, even though I had no idea why he had entered my room in that state of undress. He smiled and asked:

"Why are you hiding? What do you think I'm going to do?"

I had no reply. All I knew was my father shouldn't be in my room in his rather loose underwear. Worse yet, something rod-like was pushing his underwear out at his groin. I felt scared but didn't know why.

He came over and stood beside my bed for a second. His groin, now only a couple of feet from my face, was directly in my line of sight. I felt nauseous and was sweating profusely.

"I ... I've got to get ready for school!" I stammered. "I'm going to be late!" I started to get up but he stopped me with his hand on my chest.

"Relax," he soothed. "You have plenty of time. I just want to show you something."

Before I could protest further, he pulled away the blankets, gave me a quick once-over top to bottom (I was in a short summer nightie) and climbed into my bed, straddling me, but not touching me.

"Put both your hands up on your pillow near your head!" He ordered. I hesitated, so he grabbed my hands, extending my arms onto my pillow, and held them there.

"What are you so scared of?" he asked. My heart was pounding in my chest and the nausea was choking me. What was he going to do? I couldn't reply. I was terrified. He continued, his voice still soothing but his face more threatening:

"Daddy just wants to show you something, teach you something. You like to learn, don't you?"

I still couldn't speak. I just looked at his face trying not to cry.

"Oh, come on!" he demanded. "Relax! I just want to show you how defenseless a girl is when a man pins her down as I'm doing now. I want you to try and fight me. Try to push me off as if you were trying to get away."

I hesitated a moment, afraid he was about to hit me, but the look in his eyes warned me to do as he asked. I knew his temper well by now, his flash rages, the sting of his huge hand on my cheek. I began to struggle against him, trying to free my pinned hands. As I struggled, he pinned me down harder.

"Try harder!" he commanded. "Try to wriggle out from under me!"

I started wriggling, desperately attempting to get out from under him. Now he put his full weight on top of my body, still keeping my hands pinned, and all the time coaxing me. I could feel that hard rod rammed against my privates. It was bruising me.

"That's it!" he panted. "Now you've got it!" He seemed excited, his breaths coming fast as I continued to struggle. "Good girl!"

I stopped fighting. It was pointless. I couldn't get away. I started to cry. What would he do next! He paused, looked at my face wet with tears, and let out a frustrated, slightly annoyed, "Arrrggghhh!" Mercifully, he pulled himself up and let my hands go.

"Hey," he said, "what are the tears for? What are you so afraid of? I didn't hurt you, did I?"

"No daddy..." I replied meekly. "I just got scared."

"Well, that's exactly what I was trying to teach you! I just wanted you to see how hard it is to get away from a man. A woman is defenseless against us. You're just not strong enough to fight us off if we want to do something with you."

I didn't want to ask what that something was but I felt it must have something to do with that rod-like thing that had pushed up his underwear. I was still that naive, that innocent! I looked into his face. He was smiling nicely now and getting off my bed. When he was smiling, his was a handsome face, not threatening, a face that invited trust, belief that everything was okay. He really wasn't trying to do anymore than teach me, prepare me for the dangers out there in that big world...was he?

"Daddy? I stammered, "you wouldn't do anything to me like that, would you?" I still had no idea what THAT was or what I was really asking about. But he did.

"Of course not, my love," he replied gently now, reassuring me. "I'm your father. My job is to protect you. That's why I did this...to teach you. Now, hurry up and get ready for school."

I scrambled out of the bed that, despite his reassurance, no longer seemed a safe place, feeling like school had already begun for the day. I wanted so much to believe him, to trust him, but for some reason I felt dirty and didn't know why. I ran to the bathroom and tried to scrub my face and hands clean but the dirt wouldn't come off. The morning's first lesson had left me weak, drained and feeling soiled. I was also very confused and completely unconvinced that what had just happened was all about how defenseless a girl is against a man.

CHAPTER 9. INCEST 101

My reservations about my father's intentions grew over the next few weeks, months. I really don't know how long it was from my first lesson till graduation in Incest 101, but I came to hate waking up on a weekday morning.

Every morning I would tiptoe out of bed trying to avoid squeaky floorboards, hopeful that just this once, I could somehow sneak out of the house without hearing my father's voice calling from the front bedroom:

"You awake, kitten? Come to daddy..."

And not once did I get away with it. I had to go to his bed where he would pull back the covers and wordlessly demand, all the time smiling, that I climb in for that morning's lesson.

Weak with loathing for what would come next, filled with dread of how in depth this morning's "lesson" would be, I'd obey. Resistance was futile. That only brought on his rage and I couldn't take the verbal lashings that bit by bit were reducing me to a nothing, mentally and spiritually. They left me no choice but to oblige.

As I slipped under the covers, my mind went to some other place: I could hear his voice. I could feel his touch. But my body and my mind were divorced for that half hour while he explored how far he would get each morning.

Balloons

At times like this I dream of balloons
That lift me way up high
Above your storm of angry words
That make me want to cry

Adrift on powder puffs of clouds
With sunlight on my skin
I sense the peace of a great beyond
I never feel within

I no longer see your frightening face
Nor feel your loathsome touch
I float far above this shameful world
I've come to fear so much

If only balloons could keep me there
Keep me from tumbling down
Back to that place I thought I'd left
Alone there on the ground

©*Viga Boland, 2013*

He began his morning lessons slowly, always telling me he was just trying to teach me about sex, alternately reassuring me he wouldn't hurt me and insisting all fathers did this to their daughters. He even suggested it was a rite of passage in many cultures, that it was only natural that fathers be the first to open that very tight passage inside a woman for their future husbands. He drove his point home by insisting that one day my husband and I would thank him for the preparation he had provided! Really?

Nonetheless, it did take him time to get where he really wanted, probably because he sensed my resistance from day one. I hated the kisses which had gone from simple to deep Frenches. (To this day, French kissing repulses me). Then he began manipulating my nipples, watching them and showing me how they hardened. To him, it was a sign I was enjoying what he was doing. Enjoyment? Ha! All I really felt was the roughness of his fingers hurting me. Bit by bit, morning after morning, he'd let his hands roam over the rest of my body. The more he sensed me moving away, pulling my knees tightly together so he couldn't get to where I now knew he wanted to go, the more insistent he became, forcing my legs apart with his hands and getting angry when I resisted. Invariably, I'd start crying, reminding him that he said he'd never do anything to me. I'd bring up what little I'd been learning at school about virginity i.e. that it was precious and should be saved for that special someone, etc. But my saying things like that triggered his rage, and next thing I knew, his hand would smash across my face and he'd physically kick me out of the bed and onto the floor, shouting and guilt-tripping me with things like:

"And what am I? Am I not someone special? If I am not that someone special, then who is? Who are you saving that precious thing for! Some pimple-faced boy at school? Get out, get out you fucking whore!"

I'd run from his room, sobbing. I'd get dressed for school, all the time crying. My mind would be in utter turmoil. Confused, I'd think why was what he wanted so bad? Why didn't I just give in and save myself all this agony? How many more mornings would I have to endure this? But the other side of me kept insisting that what he wanted was so wrong! He had no right to ask that of me. He had my mother for that. Why wasn't he getting it from her? Why didn't he just leave me alone? More than ever, I'd tell myself that I must be a really bad person for God to let this happen to me. And for that matter, where was God anyway? Why wasn't he helping me? So much for "suffer the little children to come to me". After all, I was still a child, not yet out of Grade 8!

I'd watch him leaving for work, still shouting angry expletives at me as he closed the front door, telling me what an unloving daughter I was and how I was just another fucking cunt like my mother. Thoroughly guilt-tripped for being a disobedient child but not understanding why I was a "cunt" or "whore" or even what those words meant, I'd leave for school, shaking, crying and wishing I were dead.

Children of incest
Used, Accused
Refused and abused

Deceived
Not believed
They grieve unrelieved

They try
They cry
They die with each lie

Never given any choices
Faceless children
Silent voices

©Viga Boland 2013

CHAPTER 10. ADVANCED EDUCATION

By now, you must be wondering where was mom while all this was happening. As I mentioned earlier, unfortunately for me, mom left for work every morning at 6am. She had no idea what took place after she left. And sadly, as the next ten years or so proved to me, and as my father kept drumming into my brain, she wouldn't have believed me even if I had told her. So daddy's dirty little secret remained safe for him and became a living daymare and nightmare for me.

At school, I was to all others, just another kid in the playground, albeit a lonely one and certainly not one of the popular girls. I was the tallest in my class in Grade 8, not the shorty I ended up as, and I was one of the "brainers" as we called those who got good marks back then. Being a "brainer" wasn't an option for me: ever since I'd started school, my father was super tough on me regarding homework, good marks and good reports. I didn't dare bring home anything less than straight "A's" in everything or I got bashed around the head or had my face smashed into the table over my workbook if I didn't get some math concept or spelled a word wrong.

"Daddy ... I did really well on my math test this week. Look!"

Excited, I handed him the test.

"It's only 98%," he said, handing it back to me. I was crestfallen. Whatever I achieved was never good enough.

"What's good about that? It should be 100%. You'll need to do better than that, my girl, if you're ever to get anywhere!"

His daughter had to be the best, the smartest of all their friends' children and you would see his pride swell whenever they discussed how their kids were doing in school. To him, their children, mostly girls, were silly airheads. To me, they were happy free spirits who had friends and nice clothes, who enjoyed parties and listening to rock'n roll, who read teen mags, drooled over cute guys and talked about their latest crush at school. I had nothing to add to their conversations: what was uppermost in my mind and was eating into my heart, soul and spirit was something I couldn't share with anyone.

I was filled with shame and self-loathing and was so very much alone. More and more what I had learned from Desi, Mrs. Nastrom and that dead kitten cemented itself in my mind: there were many things in life that I would want and couldn't have, and much of what I got was what I didn't want. Even my kitten had the warmth of my arms. I had no arms to comfort me.

I don't really know how long it was before my father finally got into what he really wanted...and I mean "into" literally. I do remember that he tried prodding my vagina with that hard rod of his a bit more every morning, but I'd cry out so much he'd back off, at least at first. He'd remind me, almost kindly sometimes, that what he was doing was quite normal so I shouldn't be scared but some girls are tighter than others. He didn't know that I'd also read that when a woman doesn't want a man to violate her, she can, and will, close right up, making it nearly impossible for the man to get in there. So that is what I'd try to do: squeeze myself shut as much as possible down there. I wanted to make it so hard for him that he'd give up. But he never did. Rather, with each attempt, he became more determined, more furious at my constant resistance:

"What's wrong with you, for heaven's sake! You're big enough down there now. You're not a baby any more! You should be wanting this yourself! Why do you fight me so much? If you'd just relax, you'd make it easier for both of us! Now relax!"

Relax? Make it easier for him? No way! I should be wanting this myself? The very thought of him inside me made me want to vomit! I'm not a baby any more? No, I wasn't, but I was his daughter! What didn't he get about that? Why couldn't he see it as I did?

By the time he succeeded, my mind had trained itself to block out most of what transpired every dreaded morning. That was the only way to get through a school day. I'd listen to teachers, do my lessons, play with the girls at recess, day-dream about Victor who sat a few seats down from me and had eyes only for Betty (whom I simultaneously admired and envied) and braced myself as I walked home alone to what had become a prison.

Thankfully, just as Mom left for work before Dad did, she also came home earlier. That was an okay part of my afternoon as she and I loved to watch American Bandstand together. We'd grab a snack and eagerly watch our favorite teens dancing around the floor to the great 50's hits. We knew all their names and waited for them to wander into the camera's eye.

"Look, mom! There's Carol Scaldeferri. Oh, look what she's wearing today. She's so beautiful!" Carol was a dark-haired beauty who reminded us of Elizabeth Taylor. She was always immaculately coiffed and dressed. Mom was nuts about her and young Billy Cook.

"There, Viga. There's Billy! Oh, how that boy can dance! Just like Fred Astaire! He's with Bonnie, the blond bombshell. Gosh, she's a pretty one!"

And so we'd go on, sharing something we both enjoyed and dreamed we had. These young people looked so happy, carefree, enjoying life, so unlike either mom or myself. But we never talked about our lives. I think, just like me, mom was living vicariously through those teens, remembering the young woman she was once, before dad: a young woman who loved to party. She had been beautiful, with a sensuous face and a short but curvy body, and men were attracted to her like bees to a flower. But just as Dad was doing to me, he had long ago kicked the life out of her and made sure she always knew that he was lord and master. He ruled us both with his huge fists, his easily triggered temper, his uncontrolled rages, his incessant demands, and the brutal words and filthy names he hurled at us like knives. We were cut, covered in stings and black with bruises, physically and mentally. And as he wanted, we were completely powerless against him.

And so it was that one morning, he finally got inside me. The pain was horrific: it shot through my loins and all the way up to my stomach. I lurched in agony. I wanted to hurl. Sweat broke out all over me and somewhere in all that, my mind cried out: "What did I do to deserve this!" I couldn't bear to look at his face breathing hard against mine: I was utterly repulsed by it. I couldn't stomach the thought that this was my father inside me. It was so wrong! I didn't zone out this time. I couldn't with all the turmoil in my head. All I kept thinking was how could he do this to me, his daughter?

And to think I had actually believed him when he said he'd never touch me this way. He was my father! That thought kept playing over and over in my mind as he forced his way deep into my body and tore into my soul. This was my Father! He had no right to do this to me! I would have trusted him with my life. Now, as I saw it, he had taken my life. He drove himself in and out of me, trying to satisfy his lust between my crying and resistance, becoming increasingly angry with me as I winced, jumped and cried out with every thrust of his weapon.

"What's wrong with you!" he shouted at me. "The worse is over now. Relax...enjoy it!" he demanded. "See, it's not that bad now, is it?"

Not that bad now? It was horrid! Enjoy it? Was he insane? As far as I was concerned, yes, he WAS insane and I had a madman inside me. And me? What of me? I was dirty, soiled, finished. I blamed myself. I hadn't fought him hard enough. I should have been able to stop him. I was cheap, a filthy little whore just like he said. And I despised myself. Life was turning into one big battle and I had just lost the biggest battle yet...and lost myself in the process. I was no longer me.

What is Child sexual abuse?

Innocence lost
An unexpected frost
Wilting still green leaves
Freezing unripe fruit

Stunted growth
Drooping limbs
Hidden raging
Premature aging

Ever alive but
Silently crying
For the child inside
So suddenly dying

©Viga Boland 2013

CHAPTER 11. NIGHTMARES

The dreams began after that: horrible, ugly, dirty dreams...nightmares. They didn't come every night as each morning was nightmare enough. But they recurred over the years, even long after I'd left home, got married, had my children ... even sometimes now.

What I'm about to relate is unpleasant, graphic and not for weak stomachs. Feel free to skip over it.

In the first of these nightmares, I need to go to the toilet, desperately. I run. The only toilet I can find is a porta-potty. I relieve myself and look around for paper to wipe myself. I find a roll on the floor but it's covered in excrement: foul smelling, horrible. But I must wipe myself somehow. I try to unravel it, hoping there's a clean piece inside. Instead, I get the shit all over my hands. Now I'm trying to wipe it off on the walls: it's smearing everywhere and I can't get it off. Again I reach for the toilet roll, but now it's covered in blood, menstrual blood, dark and clotted and sticky. It too sticks to my fingers, mixing with the crap. I panic, start crying. How can I get out of this porta-potty with blood and excrement all over me now? It's on my fingers, my arms, my dress. Everyone will see me. I don't know what to do! I wake up, covered in sweat, my heart racing.

What does it all mean? I figured it out some years back.

The dreams eased after I realized what they meant. It's amazing how vivid and detailed the dreams were and still are now, over 50 years later. Like so many others who have suffered sexual abuse, the actual events are often a blur, quite fuzzy, so much so in fact that for many years I questioned whether any of this had really happened. Maybe I had just imagined it all? But if that were true, why do the memories keep surfacing like buried bones beneath dirt? That image, bones beneath dirt, was the dominant one in my other recurring dream. It's not as revolting as the first one, but whenever I had it, it disturbed me even more.

In this dream, I am in the basement of a very old house. Something is buried there but I don't know what. I have a little shovel and am digging around. I feel frightened of what I might find though I have no idea what it might be. Suddenly, I find it. It's a body, or more accurately, a skeleton. I jump away in horror. I'm terrified. How did this body get here? Whose body is it? I'm panicking now.

Suddenly my father is there in another part of the cellar. There's a mound of dirt in front of him. The light is behind him so that his face is in shadow. I cannot make out his features but I know it is him. He puts his fingers to his lips and warns me to "Shush!" I begin to protest and start to cry. Whose body is this? Are there more than this one? What is under that mound in front of him? Who put the bodies here? Did he? Did I? Did we murder someone?

He orders me to toss the dirt back onto the skeleton and hurry up. Sobbing, I do as I'm told. I'm so frightened, not so much of him this time but of what I may have done. Again he tells me to hurry up. As I finish, he warns me to never tell anyone what we found. It must stay hidden. It must be kept secret. My heart aches with the knowledge that there is a skeleton buried under the dirt in our home. I live in fear it will be unearthed and authorities will work out that my father and I murdered someone and I will spend my life in prison for something I don't remember doing. But I do as he tells me: I never tell anyone. But I now know whose skeleton was under that dirt: mine.

CHAPTER 12. THE RATIONALE

The years following that traumatic day are actually quite a blur, even more so than the ones that preceded it. All that sticks out in my mind now are incidences that cemented the hopelessness of my situation. Each event convinced me I would never escape this role my father had selected for me: I would be his mistress forever. I fantasized about escaping but I was too terrified of him to even try. I completely believed that if I were to try, that other mound of dirt in that cellar in my dream would indeed be my body and he would have put it there.

He also very cleverly began brainwashing me. He knew how to talk, how to manipulate my feelings and fears: if I were to tell anyone, who would believe me? After all, everyone who met him found him handsome, friendly and quite charming, a father who cared greatly about his wife and daughter. To all the world he looked like a model father, albeit a strict one. So who would believe me?

He'd reach for a cigarette after his morning dose of sex with his daughter, and before he'd let me go and get ready for school, he'd deliberate a little more about the psychology and morality of incest:

"After all, what is so wrong about what we are doing?" he'd muse. "This is just a man and woman having sex, right?" Was he trying to convince himself or me? When I wouldn't respond one way or another, he'd try another angle:

"Don't you realize what a wonderful thing you are doing for this family, for your mother and me? If it weren't for you, I'd probably be out having affairs with other women. And what might happen then? You could be the cause of our family breaking up if I fell for someone else."

This soother was his justification for what he was doing. He'd drum it into my head that I was just being a really good daughter to mom and dad and keeping our family together. Wasn't that a great thing? I had no reply. The way I felt, I just wished that he would indeed find another woman and leave me the hell alone!

As for his argument as to why I shouldn't tell my mother, I bought into it, not just because I reasoned he was right, i.e. who would believe me...but also because I simply wouldn't and couldn't hurt my mother with the truth. Furthermore, what would she think of me? Would she believe, as he insisted she would, that I had seduced him? That it was me who wanted and asked for this? I couldn't bear the thought she might think that. She already didn't seem to like me all that much. This would make her hate me and I already had enough hate for myself for the both of us. So no, instead I would put up and shut up and give myself to him for breakfast every morning for years to come.

Author's note:

Simon Denman of the website, ***READERS IN THE KNOW***, has done a marvelous reading of this chapter in his podcast at this link below:

http://www.readersintheknow.com/podcast/29

He has captured the emotion I felt as I wrote this section and what I felt as a child incredibly well. If you have time to listen, please do.

CHAPTER 13: UGLY

We lived in that ground floor flat until I graduated from Grade 8. When I wasn't being used by my dad to satisfy his sexual appetite or as a battering ram for his temper, school and a part-time job working as a shelf-stocker at Loblaws were my diversions, and my only real sources of pleasure.

I wasn't one of the popular girls at school, thanks to my quick temper and generally uninviting appearance I guess. Popular girls, like my friend Betty, were pretty and wore fashionable clothing. I was plain ugly ... at least in my opinion. Surprisingly, I was the tallest girl in my Grade 8 class, (though I never grew taller than 5' 3") but that didn't give me any edge with the other kids. Nor did the fact that I was a "browner" i.e. got good marks. That made me even less liked. But worst of all, as I saw it, were my looks. My hair was unruly. My clothes were the cheapest mom could buy. My shoes were "practical", selected for durability not style by my father, who was ever mindful of how we spent our money. And as my father constantly reminded me, and would for years to come, no boys would ever be interested in me because I was so ugly. So wasn't I lucky to have him... he loved me, ugly and all.

I bought into his thinking, so it came as a surprise to me when a tall good-looking boy named Richard, started hanging around after school waiting to walk me home after I finished my tasks as classroom monitor. His attention confused me, in light of what my father was saying about me. But Richard was funny and friendly and very popular with the girls, so I lapped up his attention. One day he suggested I go to a movie with him on the coming Saturday. I panicked at the suggestion. I knew my father would never allow me to date. I wasn't quite 14 yet. So Richard, the charmer, got my phone number and called me that evening to ask my dad's permission. Dad answered the phone and I watched his face contort with rising anger as poor Richard asked to talk to me.

"And just what do you want to talk to her about?" bellowed my dad.

Richard replied and Dad's voice was loud and threatening as he said to Richard:

"And just who are you? What is your last name? And who gave you the right to phone my daughter?"

As Richard was replying, my stomach was doing flip- flops and my heart was in my throat. I could almost see Richard cowering at the other end of the line. I have no idea what he said to my dad, but my father ended the conversation with a few threats that Richard best stay away from me and he would be sorry if my father ever saw him speaking or walking with me and he was never to call our house again. Bam! Dad slammed the phone down. He looked at me and I braced myself for a beating or at least a verbal ear bashing. What he gave me instead was a smirk, a grinning gargoyle face. He looked hideous and frightening all at once.

"Well, that got rid of him eh?" he smirked, anger rising in his voice. "Who the hell does he, this Richard, think he is, calling you? And how come he got your number? Do you talk to him at school?"

Panic was welling up in me. I didn't dare tell him the truth. "No...no," I lied. "I don't talk to him. He's not even in my class. I...I don't know how he got my number. Maybe...from one of my friends?"

I don't know if he believed me but he just started laughing and smirking again. I realized that this had all been a power trip for him, a chance to show me that there would be no more Richards in my life, as he said:

"Well, I showed him, didn't I! Stupid little punk thinking he can call you. He's never met a real man yet. I showed him how I deal with punks!"

Then his look turned stern again. His voice carried unspoken threat as he finished the incident with:

"Don't ever let that happen again! No boys! No phone calls! No talking to boys at school! Do you understand!"

That wasn't a question. It was a demand that had only one answer.

"Yes, daddy..." I said meekly. But deep inside me, my own rage and resentment rose. There might be future Richards but he wouldn't know about them. I would learn to lie to survive in this prison he was building around me.

The next "Richard" in my life was George, or rather Jurgen. My father never knew of him. I was learning to cover all my activities and feelings about the opposite sex.

Jurgen was also a shelf-stocker at Loblaws. I was trying to put some baby food jars on the topmost shelf one Saturday and nearly dropped an entire load when I couldn't quite reach it. Suddenly, a tall, slim blond god saved a disaster of smashing baby food jars from happening: Jurgen miraculously appeared beside me, grabbed the box, and stopped the display from toppling. I turned to him and all I could see were smiling green eyes and a huge grin on the most handsome male face I'd ever seen. He winked at me, laughing, then put his hands on my waist to lift me off the step-stool I was using. Electricity shot through me, head to toe at his touch. I was awestruck! I must have looked like Betty Hutton when she played Annie Oakley in the movie, "Annie Get Your Gun" and she first saw Wild Bill Hickok. He was so gorgeous!

"Looks like you need to grow a little more, eh?" he said, winking at me again. "When did you get hired?"

I couldn't reply. My throat was dry. I couldn't take my eyes off him. My face was flushing and my body tingling. What the hell was this!

"What's the matter?" he taunted me, smiling all the while. "Cat got your tongue?"

I have no idea what I finally said, but as he walked off with a wave, still laughing, my eyes took in every inch of his slim athletic body, the slight curl in his hair and the confident swagger in his carriage. I was in love!

Unfortunately, or maybe fortunately for me, given my home situation, Jurgen didn't see me as anything more than that kid who stocks the baby food shelves, someone to poke a little fun at now and then to see her blush. He was always cracking jokes or playing tricks on me, then asking why I turned red so easily. But despite it all, I adored every bit of attention he gave me. I was somehow more aware of myself as a female part of the species, more aware of my own body and its odd mix of sensations and emotions. I felt alive when I was at my job. I felt like my life was normal and what was happening at home was in some other world, not mine. And as my father released his sexual appetite in me each morning before I left for school, I closed my eyes and ran happily through sunny fields, pursued by a laughing Jurgen with smiling green eyes.

Despite my father's insistence, and my growing acceptance, that indeed, I was ugly and no man other than him would ever want me, there was one other young man who worked in the veggie department at Loblaws who apparently thought otherwise. Because I only had eyes for Jurgen, I never saw Bill's cheery greetings of "Hi Gorgeous!" as anything more than annoying. He always had a huge smile for me too, but he wore thick glasses, a bit Buddy Hollyish, and had no sex appeal at all (not that I recognized that was what he was missing at that point).

One day, when I was being trained to work on the cash registers, the head checker caught me staring jealously at a curvaceous, pretty blond who had been transferred from another shop. Jurgen was laughing and joking with her as she stocked the baby food shelves. She was flirting back, wiggling her bottom at him and giving him the come-on. I was dying inside. She had taken my job and now she wanted my blond god!

"Eyes on the register!" chided the head-checker, laughing at me. (Seems people were always laughing at me for something!) "Stop dreaming about Jurgen," she advised kindly. "He's too old for you and he's not really interested in girls."

Sure could have fooled me the way he was flirting with blondie!

"I know him and his family," she explained. "He's a brilliant student. Spends all his time studying. He's planning to go into medicine when he graduates. He has no time for girls, especially one still in Grade 8!" She laughed again at how preposterous that idea was. She was probably right. I was too young, too ugly, and quite awkward falling off step stools.

"If you want a boyfriend... " she continued, "why don't you give Bill a chance?"

"Bill?" I stammered, looking over at Bill who was staring at me the way I'd stare at Jurgen. "Do you mean HIM?" I asked, indicating Bill with a shift of my eyes in his direction.

"Sure! Why not? He's been carrying the torch for you since you started here. Didn't you ever notice? He's crazy for you!"

I couldn't believe what I was hearing. For one, no, I hadn't really noticed since I only had eyes for Jurgen. But more to the point, Dad had told me no man would want me. I was ugly. I was incredulous at the preposterous idea someone could find me attractive. That's why as much as I wanted Jurgen, I understood I wasn't attractive to him. He'd like pretty girls like blondie. But now it appeared someone did find me pretty too. Could my father be wrong?

While I still had no interest in poor Bill who, according to the head checker, apparently pined and sighed every time I walked by, I suddenly felt just a little better about myself. At least the ugliness I felt inside wasn't as obvious on the outside as I thought.

CHAPTER 14: THE GRADUATE

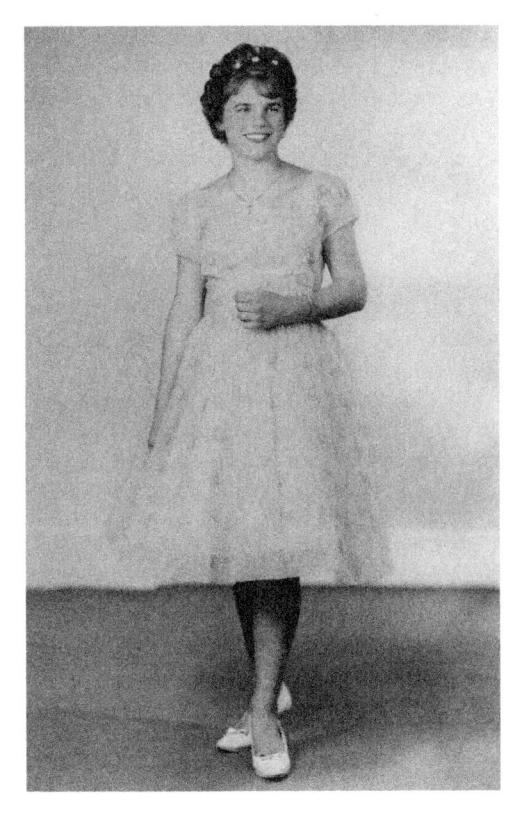

My graduation from Grade 8, like most things in my life, was a non-event for my parents as they were both at work during the ceremonies. But at least they did spring for a pretty floral green dress with a big skirt and for a change, I felt a little less like a creep when I walked up to accept my diploma. But the good feeling didn't last all that long once my father got home and asked how it went. He seemed to be in a good mood so I babbled on about the ceremony and all the excitement. He made some comment about how I was now growing up and asked if I was ready to take on a more adult role in my decisions, etc. I wasn't sure what he was driving at but he was being so pleasant and interested in me for something other than sex that I suddenly felt bold enough to ask if I could attend a grad party being hosted by one of the girls.

"Where is this party?" he asked, smiling.

"At Sophie's house. She just lives up a couple of blocks from here," I replied, not fully showing how eager I was to go as I wasn't sure if he was genuinely considering letting me attend. But he had said something about me making my own decisions now. So maybe this was one he'd let me make.

"And do you really want to go?" He was still smiling. "Oh yes!" I replied, perhaps a little too enthusiastically. "Why?"

I didn't know how to answer that and couldn't see why he would ask. After all, it was my graduation and someone had invited me to a party. Why wouldn't I want to go? What was I supposed to say? What was he expecting?

"Well..." I started hesitantly, choosing my words carefully as something in his eyes was making me suddenly wary. "Well, I've never gone to a class party and all the kids will be there and I most likely will only see a few of them again as we're all going to different high schools...and...I'd just like to go to say good-bye one last time? "

By now, his face had changed. Something was twitching in a corner of his mouth, like I'd seen before when he was getting angry about something.

"And what will all the kids be doing there?"

"Well, I don't know daddy. I've never been to a party before. Just talking, listening to music. Maybe dancing a bit...I don't know..."

He looked at me oddly for a second then suddenly said, "Okay...you can go."

I couldn't believe it! He was letting me go to a party. I felt such a rush of joy I ran over to him, hugged him, kissed him and repeated over and over "Oh, thank you Daddy! Thank you so much! I love you Daddy!"

I turned to go to my bedroom to get dressed for the party but his voice stopped me.

"Where are you going?"

I looked at him blankly. He was no longer smiling. He looked like he was simmering, a bit like the transition that took place in Dr. Jekyll's face as he mutated into Mr. Hyde.

"Uh...I'm...uh going to get changed for the party... " I stammered.

"Oh really?" he said. His voice was sarcastic, his face ugly, twitching. "Well, I've changed my mind. You're not going!" he yelled.

My face flushed. What was this? I stood rooted on the spot. I couldn't move. He continued...

"What do you think?" he asked me, "...that I'm going to let you go to some party where there will be boys... maybe that RICHARD... " He spat out his name like it was poison. "And that you are going to dance with them and let them put their arms around you? Maybe steal a kiss or two? What are you thinking!"

By now his face was filled with rage. "No way! Not my daughter acting like a some cheap whore. You're staying home! How dare you ask that of me! I bought you a dress for graduation. Wasn't that enough? You want too much all the time. I give you a finger; you take a hand! You ungrateful child! Go to your room and don't come back in here until you're ready to apologize!"

I retreated meekly to my room, fell on my bed and sobbed. What on earth had I done wrong? What was so bad about wanting to go to a grad party with some friends? Why was I an "ungrateful child". I was giving him all he wanted from me and what was he giving me back? His rod in the morning? Forgive my crudeness, but that's how I felt and I am being honest in recounting the circumstances of my incestuous situation. The only one turning me into a whore was him. And now, I felt more like a whore than ever. I'd been paid off with a new dress. Wasn't I the lucky one!

He had baited me. It wasn't the last time he would do so. Over the years as I passed through adolescence and finally into adulthood, he would probe my real feelings time and again, and I'd fall into his trap over and over. I so wanted to believe that my "daddy", my "real" father would re-emerge and be what I thought a father should be: someone I could love and trust, someone with whom I could share my hopes, dreams and plans honestly and without fear of reprisal or condemnation. But that person disappeared the day my father made me his secret wife.

THE LEGACY of ABUSE

Anger rages deep
Demons never sleep

Memories weaken but never leave
Hearts ache and forever grieve

This is the legacy of abuse
For which there's never any excuse

The adult grows, ever trying
To comfort the child inside who's crying

This is the legacy of abuse
Families living in denial

The abuser walks free to hurt again
The victim remains ever on trial

©Viga Boland 2012

CHAPTER 15: HIGH SCHOOL

High School! Oh, how happy I was! We had moved out of the city into Etobicoke, still a fairly young suburb at the time. I had to take streetcars and buses to get to Loretto College School in the heart of Toronto on time and it was a full hour's trip from home. That meant my father couldn't rape me each morning: there simply wasn't enough time. Joy! Finally God was looking out for me after all and answering all those prayers I had thought He was too busy to hear when He had so many others with bigger problems than mine to attend to. I thanked that lucky star I wished on every night believing this move would put an end to my father's sexual abuse of me and maybe, just maybe, I could become a normal teen after all.

My joy and my reprieve from my father's lust was short-lived. Since he could no longer have his way with me in the morning, he found another way. This came unwittingly courtesy of my poor mother's great evening fatigue. After 5 a.m. starts to get to work at Christie's Biscuits on the Lakeshore and eight hours of factory work, she'd begin nodding off shortly after supper in front of the TV. It took very little, seemingly concerned coaxing from my father, to get her to slip into bed for a little nap. That would give him all the time he needed with me and he made sure it was easy by always insisting I sit beside him, covered by a blanket, on that fold-out bed chesterfield that we had to have ready for him when he returned from work. I'd watch mom amble off, inwardly screaming "Don't go, mom," tension flooding me, wishing for once she'd stay awake and make it impossible for him. But she never did.

Like a wolf in wait, you could almost see him licking his chops in anticipation. All I felt was increasing nausea and dread. What if mom suddenly walked in while he was doing it? He'd wait, ears perked to hear if she might return, and once he felt secure, he'd roll toward me, pull my stiff and resisting body against his hardness and begin to rub. He'd tear hungrily at my underwear, struggling to get it off without making the chesterfield creak too much, getting more annoyed with me for not taking it off earlier to make it easier for him. Somehow I still foolishly believed after two years that by resisting him he'd give up. Or maybe I was hoping suddenly we'd hear mom and he'd have to stop. So I'd lie there, ever tensed, ever on the alert for mom, filled with nausea and just wishing he'd get it over and done with so I could get off that hated chesterfield and slip away to my room.

When he was done, he'd stroke my face tenderly, almost lovingly, telling me what a good girl I was, saying how much he loved me, reminding me how I was keeping their marriage together and that I was so good for his stress. Couldn't I see how much doing this calmed him down after a hard day's work and made him nice to be with again? And it wasn't that bad really, was it? After all, I should be used to it by now. I'd nod my head in agreement as I knew that would keep him calm. It was what he expected me to say and I was all for peace at any price by now. But what I wanted to say he didn't want to hear. It would have inflamed him. No! It wasn't easier. He felt calmer but I felt sicker, filthier, uglier with every session. I may have been his sedative, but he was the reverse for me: the ultimate stressor that filled me with fear and loathing, pumped up my adrenaline, made my head ache with heightened blood pressure and brought on those shit-filled nightmares when I was finally safe in bed.

Bed. Safe in bed. That's what most children want to believe bed is: a place to snuggle under the blankets with a favorite toy or when older, a good book until sleep enfolds them safely in its arms, secure from harm while the brain sorts through the body's day. For me, sleep was rarely a peaceful exit from the day at any age after the sexual abuse began. If the nightmares didn't come to waken me, my father did, especially after I turned sixteen and could drive them home from the adult parties which my father insisted I attend. But I'm jumping ahead a bit too quickly here. So let me backtrack to my transition to high school where I truly began to understand how different my life was from those of my friends.

Loretto College School was, of course, a Catholic school. There was really only one reason I attended the college instead of a regular public high school: there were no boys there. No way would my father risk the chance I'd be around the opposite sex. After all, I had him, didn't I? What more did I need?

Even better in his opinion was the fact that we wore these dark navy serge uniforms, so dark they were almost as black as the habits the teaching nuns wore. They did nothing for our figures so I couldn't attract the opposite sex traveling back and forth by public transport, and given my inherent ugliness, who would look at me anyway? The uniforms came with detachable hard plastic collars kept together by a clip-on bow. The plastic bit into my neck and gave me a red ring around the collar that chafed at the end of the day, especially in early summer. We also had plastic cuffs at the ends of our sleeves that simply wouldn't stay up so I was constantly adjusting them. I felt uncomfortable, lumpy with adolescent "baby fat". Every day was a bad hair day, and with food crumbs that always seem to drop and stick to the serge, I looked disheveled and unkempt ... at least to myself. I'd go to the girls' washrooms at recess and look enviously at the other girls' reflections in the mirrors. They had pretty faces, nicely cut hair, and were always laughing, joking around and giggling about the cute guys they'd met at last week's Friday night Youth Club dances. I felt so awkward by comparison, so left out, so different from them all and so far removed from the kinds of lives they had that I almost wondered if my family and I were aliens from another planet. These kids just had nothing in common with me and what was going on in my home.

But oh, how I envied them and wanted to be part of their laughter and lives and Friday night dances. Even their uniforms seem to fit well: their cuffs didn't keep sliding down their wrists and they had no red rings around their necks. And most of them had 2-3 uniforms so they didn't wear the same one day in and day out and get crumbs all over them. Mine even smelled of my perspiration: I had a big problem with underarm BO in the hot weather, thanks to my permanent state of nervousness, but I only had the one uniform. So even bathing every morning didn't help by noon. My sense of being ugly, dirty, undesirable even as a girlfriend just grew and grew in those first few months of high school. And given no-one tried to make friends with me, it was easy to conclude no-one really wanted me around anyway. As bad as my father was, at least he talked to me when he was being just a father.

I dealt with my lonely feelings of being different and not being someone others found repulsive as I always had: I plunged myself into my schoolwork, was a model student, paid attention in class and pleased my teachers and parents. Let's change that to my father. My mother never had much to say about anything. As dad often reminded her, she was just a stupid farm girl who barely finished Grade 4, so her opinions didn't count and she didn't know enough about anything to advise or otherwise. As the years went on, she so believed what he fed her about herself that even if she suddenly sprung to my defense when he was bashing me around or being overly severe, he'd remind her of her ignorance and insist that anything going on between him and me in any respect was none of her business and she was to stay out of it. Did she know about the sexual abuse? I really don't think so. Did she even suspect? Not sure but I doubt it. I hid his dirty secret that well and he was so clever and manipulative with his words and with his ability to talk at us both for so long and so hard, that we'd both space out and let him rave on. It was just too tiring to argue or oppose. Like I said earlier, it was peace at any price for me both then, and to a lesser degree, for the rest of my life.

Not much stands out in my mind about my first year of high school beyond what I've just written. The best part about Grade 9 was the freedom I felt as I left the house each morning. Even something as simple as waiting for the bus was liberating: dad wasn't looking over my shoulder! Despite having next to no friends, it felt good to walk the school halls and attend classes without asking for his permission to do everything. I relished the long ride home, changing street cars and buses, watching other people, looking at how they dressed, wondering what I'd look like wearing fashionable clothes and having nice hair. And, most liberating of all was being able to look at boys without my father shooting me a scathing look or suddenly, out of nowhere, giving me a box in my ears or a whack over the back of my head. Oh yes, he'd do that right in public if he saw me even stealing a glance at a guy walking by. In fact, he'd do it even if I didn't look at him.

I remember clearly walking up the street to the shops with dad one day. He was talking about something or other I'd already tuned out. Someone walked by us and instantly, Dad stopped what he was saying and in a snarky, sarcastic voice goaded me with:

"So did he appeal to you?"

I came out of a semi-coma and asked: "Who?"

My response angered him. "Don't bullshit me! Who? That guy that just walked by! Don't pretend you weren't looking at him!"

I turned to my father, fear gathering in my gut and throat, as I replied honestly:

"Papa ... I never saw any guy ... "

Dad gave me a quick belt across the back of my head and shouted: "Don't lie to me, you whore! I saw you looking at him! What were you looking at? His pimply face? Were you trying to see what was in his pants?! You filthy cunt! You think I don't know what's on your mind?"

I was so shocked, I couldn't speak. Tears sprung to my eyes, more because of what he said than the blow to the back of my head. I was innocent. I hadn't even seen the guy. I'd kept my eyes straight ahead and was my usual zoned-out self when my Dad was yapping on about something. And here I was being accused of something I hadn't done or never even thought about.

My father was strangling me, confining me, putting bars on my windows to the world a bit more every day. No wonder going to school was the best thing about my day: for nine hours or so, I was away from the house and him. I had nine hours to look at, feel, and think what I wanted. The rest of the time, I lived a lie, showing my father the face he wanted to see, telling him what he wanted to hear, smiling at him when I wanted to spit at him, and dreading facing another evening of lying beside him on the fold-out, waiting for mom to take her nap, so he could get his rocks off and then tell me what a good daughter I was for being good to daddy.

CHAPTER 16: GIN & MILK

By Grade 10, those nine hours of daily freedom were helping my self-confidence grow. I still didn't like myself much, but I was less hesitant about speaking up around the other girls, at least about things I knew about. Because I excelled in Latin, and most couldn't handle it or stand it, other students sought me out for help. Sometimes the teachers would ask me to coach other students. The same applied to math and English, my favorite subjects. But when it came to history, the only place you'd find me was sliding slowly beneath my desk in the back row of the room. I hated history! It bored me stupid. By Grade 11, I was hopeless. We had the loveliest teacher, an older lady named Mrs. Culligan. She was so sweet but she spoke in such a monotone, I couldn't stay awake. It was like going to mass with the priest's voice droning on and on about something in which I had no interest or belief. (Thanks to my father, I'd lost faith a long time back). It was almost funny when the student across from me poked me in the arm as I dozed off and startled, I'd jump awake, only to drift off again a few minutes later.

It was in Grade 11 history class, that I got introduced to milk and gin. Yes, milk and gin. A pretty Hungarian girl, Melinda, used to bring a flask of milk to school that was laced with gin. I'd see her sipping it in history class. The girls around her were giggling while Mrs Culligan droned on about Greek mythology, totally oblivious to what was going on in those back two rows. I had to know why Melinda drank milk in class. Grinning, she offered it to me. I lifted my history textbook up to cover my face and took a swill. Cripe! I nearly spat it everywhere. It didn't taste like any milk I'd ever drunk! The other kids were watching my face and laughing quietly as I took another sip. Smiling stupidly, I passed it back to her and she passed it to one of the others. Suddenly, history wasn't such a bad class for me after all. I still hated the subject, but I was finally becoming just one of the girls and that felt so good.

It might seem a bit contrary to say that while my self- esteem was still super low, my self-confidence was growing, but now when I looked in the washroom mirrors, what looked back at me didn't look quite as ugly. My hair had improved, so much so in fact that one of the girls who would become one of my closest friends by Grade 12, would desperately ask me to style her hair for her each morning. She had thin wispy hair that always looked oily and wouldn't hold a curl. She also had a habit of hiding behind that hair. She looked more insecure than me, kept her eyes down or averted, always looked fearful and ashamed and was slow to smile. She was brilliant in English, dreadful in math, and like me, loved to write. Her poems were beautiful but sad. In hindsight, I feel sure that she too was harboring a dark secret. She never spoke about her home or parents except to say her father, like mine, was super strict. Neither of us were allowed to attend parties. She too seemed to have no life outside school. I think I subconsciously knew her private life was rotten but she couldn't and wouldn't share any of it with any of us. How well I understood that. We were kindred spirits and I came to love her dearly though I never learned what pained her so deeply.

Annette and I became constant companions, joined by something we knew we shared but never talked about. That's how it is when you're being abused: you keep it to yourself. Then suddenly, our twosome became a foursome. We were joined by Maryanne and Marta, both energetic, powerful girls with brilliant minds and strong personalities that shone in contrast to Annette's and mine. These two girls seemed to have no issues with anything in their lives. Both had loving families that supported everything they did. Marta was especially cheerful, always outspoken and seemingly undaunted by anything. I admired her enormously and envied her obvious freedom to be who she was and proud of it. It didn't bother her that she wasn't particularly pretty, that her hair was frizzy and even rather unruly. To Marta, looks were her last concern.

Over those last two years of senior high school, our foursome was inseparable. At school, we were always together at lunchtime and recess. Marta was terrific in sports (I was hopeless!) so we all cheered her on when she was competing. She was also fantastic at math and science, and by Grade 13, it wasn't unusual to find Marta and me staying after school working out complex trigonometry problems on the blackboard. We loved finding patterns and getting the right answers. It sometimes amazed me how good I could feel about myself at school and how horrible I felt at home.

Home. Define home. Home is where your mother rarely smiles, your father rules, and both mother and child have no say about anything at all. Home is where both mother and child wait on father hand and foot, where each thinks carefully before saying something that might bring on father's rage. Home is where you lie about your activities and dreams and keep your thoughts to yourself because to tell the truth will bring a sudden blinding vicious blow to the head or ears or an onslaught of filthy, denigrating words or a volley of hard kicks to your backside. Home is where who you are, is who your father wants you to be, not who you are. Home is where you are never yourself. Home is where you no longer know who you are. Home is the last place on earth you want to be.

I hated coming home from school. Any sense of freedom I had during the day disappeared the instant I stepped inside the duplex, even though my father wouldn't yet be home for a couple of hours. I'd get stuck into my homework immediately: it had to all be done by the time he arrived so I could take my place beside him on that hated, unfolded bed chesterfield in front of the T.V. for the rest of the evening. Mom would arrive home shortly after I did, smelling as she had for years of sweet biscuit dust and furiously rubbing her itchy nose while she bashed the meat with a meat hammer. Though she never said it, every bang of that hammer was a release of her own deep-seated anger, a hopeless rebellion against her life. Every blow echoed through my own helplessness. We were two women held captive by fear, ashamed of our weakness and disgusted by our own inability to change our lives. As dad's arrival time approached, we both sensed the tension mounting in each other, but we never talked about it. We both knew talking about our lives would most likely be a waste of time: neither of us had the courage to do anything about them.

The first thing Dad would do on arrival is search my face. His eyes would probe mine, looking for something behind the smile I'd pasted on seconds before I opened the door for him. I know he was looking to see if I was hiding something I might have done during the day that he wouldn't like. He was looking to see if I'd been faithful to him. It was almost funny: what else could I be at an all-girl school? Most of all he was looking to see if I was happy to see him. Again, that was almost funny. How could he believe that his own daughter whom he'd turned into his concubine against her will, whom he kept imprisoned by fear and shame, would be happy to see him? My life was such a lie!

Dad would ask about my day, wanting all details while mom dished out the food. If I had little to tell...how different could each school day be...he'd conclude I was hiding something and his mouth would twitch as he suppressed his anger. His interest in Mom's day was limited to "...and how was your day, love?" Like me, she had little to say and he only half listened as he turned his probing eyes back to my face. I felt nauseous every time he called her "love". How could he be so false with her? He was always telling me how he despised liars and that if he caught me lying I would regret it, that he expected full honesty at all times. So why did he call her "love"? If he loved her, then what was he doing with me? For me, he was the biggest liar of all: "Do as I say, not as I do".

One day when I was in Grade 12, I stayed back at school to help decorate the gym for the first ever school dance. All the girls were so excited: they were all bringing their boyfriends and chatting on about what they'd be wearing. I'd listen with envy: I had no boyfriend to bring and most likely wouldn't be allowed to go anyway. But at least I could help out and share their excitement. Unfortunately I missed my bus and got home about five minutes late. Dad was already home. He looked furious as I walked through the door.

"Why are you so late?" he shouted, his face red with rage.

"I...I missed my bus," I stammered.

"And why did you miss your bus?"

Dad's angry face was 6 inches from mine. I shrank back in fear, anticipating a blow to my head any second.

"I...er...stayed back to help decorate the gym for the school dance tomorrow night. I'm on the dance committee."

"What school dance? You never told me anything about a school dance. You're lying to me, aren't you!" he insisted, holding his arm up like a viper ready to strike.

I cowered in fear, becoming a little child again instead of a 16 year-old. "No daddy...no! I'm not lying!" I cried. "I'm telling you the truth. Why don't you believe me? I was decorating the gym and missed my bus!"

"You're lying!" he insisted, shouting in my face. "You know how I hate liars! Now, where were you? Who is he? What did you do? Where did you go? Was he good? Did you like it?"

He spat the questions at me and inwardly I recoiled in revulsion at what he was suggesting and fear that no matter what I said, he wouldn't believe me. Tears began pouring down my face, but from somewhere deep inside me, years of anger surged. I had done nothing wrong!

"What's the use of telling you the truth!" I screamed back at him defiantly. "I tell you the truth and you say I'm lying. I may as well lie! I'm damned if I do and damned if I don't!"

I quickly raised my arms to protect my head, expecting his punches to follow. To my shock, he seemed temporarily immobilized. His face twitched uncontrollably but he didn't strike. I could see he wanted to but was holding himself back. Still I cowered.

"Don't you ever speak to me like that again, you filthy whore! I'm your father! You do not speak like that to your father. Do you hear me? Now get out of my sight. You are not my daughter. No daughter speaks to her father like that! And remember, I hate liars!"

I ran to my room and sobbed but as the tears dried, I began to laugh to myself at the irony of what had just transpired. He hated liars, but he was the biggest liar of all. I was not his daughter. Well who had made that a reality? Not me. He was my father? Really? What kind of "father" has daily sex with his daughter instead of his wife? No, I wasn't his daughter and he wasn't my father...at least not the father I wanted, could love and with whom I could be honest. No, this was some other man, a jealous, possessive and abusive one who wanted total control of my life. But as I thought these things, one other thought warmed me: for once, I had stood up to him. As I would learn, I would pay for that bit of defiance, but for now, it was a small victory.

Not the monster under the bed

What goes on behind those doors?
Beneath the rafters, between the floors?
What fills a child with so much fright
She's afraid to go to bed at night?

It's not the monster under the bed
That fills her heart with so much dread
It's the monster that visits her room at night
And tells her "Shhh... Everything's alright"

This is the monster that she most fears
Who brings such pain and ignores her tears
The one who messes with her body and head
Not the monster under the bed

©Viga Boland, November 2012

CHAPTER 17: NOT THE MONSTER UNDER THE BED

Bed. A place of safety, warmth. The place you can't wait to go when you're so tired you can't stay awake. You climb in anticipating hours of delicious, relaxing, refreshing rest. You close your eyes and begin to drift. Suddenly, you jerk awake! What was that? You heard something, a sound outside your closed bedroom door. You wait, a knot rising in your stomach. Nothing. No more sound. Silly you. It was nothing. Must have been drifting off. No! There it is again. Your door is opening. A thin streak of light shows a shadowy figure coming into the room, now closing the door ever so quietly. Please God NO you scream inside you. Not THAT again! Please stop him! But God isn't listening.

Nausea wells up inside me. I want to throw up. I want to scream, "Leave me alone!" This thing he has now started doing is the one I've come to hate the most. My father is at the foot of my bed. He lifts the covers, finds my legs which are rigid as I try unsuccessfully to dig them deeper into the bed. I am wooden, resisting as he pulls my body to the bottom of the bed so my derrière rests on the edge. He kneels on the floor, his face level with my bottom, and roughly pushes my legs up and around his neck. My eyes have adjusted to the darkness by now. I'm fully awake, alert, tense, nauseous and helpless. He leers at me, his face a grinning drunken gargoyle. Then he buries his face in my vagina and begins "munching" as he calls it.

I am sick with loathing. The clock ticks on. I watch it as I can't bear to look at him. I feel nothing but tension and revulsion. Every so often he stops, coming up for air. He wipes his mouth and grins at me. I hope he's done. But no, he buries his face in me and continues. I watch the clock.

Finally, he stands up. I'm hoping he's finished for tonight and will let me go back to the sleep I've yet to have. It's not to be. Now he comes to the side of my bed, pulls me back up the bed by my unwilling arms, climbs on top of me and starts French kissing me. I recoil at the smell of myself still on his face, the whiskey on his breath, the whole revolting scene that I am watching with my eyes closed. It's like a movie, a horror movie that I can't wait to end. That is some other girl there. That is some other man. This couldn't be my father! Fathers don't do this to their daughters!

He is inside me now, grinding away, becoming frustrated because he can't orgasm with all that booze in him. He was stinking drunk when I drove the three of us home from the party. I had hoped he'd be too drunk to want this tonight. Mom had drunk so much she vomited as soon as we got home. Drunk as he was, he looked after her, so lovingly I wanted to puke myself. I knew what he was doing: making sure she got to bed and passed out before he came to me. I had hoped he'd fallen asleep too. But no, he had just waited, at least another hour. Then he'd come for his "midnight snack" as he called it. He thought it was fun. I had another word for it altogether: sick!

He's getting upset with himself and me now: I'm "too dry". He can't climax. He gives up at last. He climbs out of the bed, scowls, and staggers stupidly out of the room. I pull the covers up over my head, but yank them back down a second later to listen. I'm on high alert. Will he come back in and try to finish what he couldn't? Please no! I want to sleep. Every nerve in me is tingling, alert, listening, watching that door. But all is quiet. I watch the clock. Fifteen minutes since he left. I begin to relax. I start to drift. Mercifully, he won't be back this night.

CHAPTER 18: WHISKEY BREATH REASONING

My parents started taking me to their adult friends' parties once I got my license at 16. There were two reasons for this: the first was it allowed Dad to drink all he wanted now that he had me to drive them home. The second reason was he felt it was time for me to have some social life, but in a way that he could always keep an eye on me and it was unlikely I'd meet any boys at those parties. I was forbidden to date and never attended any of my school friends' parties. In fact, I never went anywhere with anyone my own age. But, according to my father, just so I couldn't complain I never had any fun, I could accompany my parents to their parties where I would enjoy the company of adults, all of whom were married and had children my age, but whose children stayed at their own homes or were out on dates with their friends.

I groaned every time we headed out for one of these parties. I knew what the night would bring: the married women would look at me wondering what the heck I was doing there instead of being out with people my own age. Their husbands would talk to me, their whiskey breaths repulsing me, their eyes forever moving down to my now ample young breasts and back to my face. To me, they were all like my father: as they talked, they were fantasizing about fondling my breasts and more. I hated most of them. I felt they knew I was my father's whore. I felt it was stamped on my brow and everyone in that room, except for my mother, could see who my father would have sex with once we got home.

I'd remain standing most of the evening, usually by the food table, feeling it was safe there. My father would never be far away. While he talked, joked and drank glass after glass, his eyes were forever watching me, watching to see if I were flirting or if any of the other dads in the room were coming on to me in any way other than just being friendly. His idea in taking me to these parties, as he explained it, was to have me accepted by their friends. They needed to see I was mature enough to be with adults and that I fit in well. When one of the more outspoken women at the party once challenged his decision to bring me along, suggesting I should be out with my own friends his response was I was too mature for the silly teenagers out there, that I didn't really like the company of young people. The woman looked at me with doubt in her eyes. My nerves jangled as she asked me right then and there in a voice that silenced the room:

"Is that true, Viga? Wouldn't you rather be at a young persons' party than here with a bunch of us parents?"

The whole room waited for my answer as my face reddened and I felt panic shoot up to my brain.

"No, I like being here," I lied. Adults were fun, more interesting.

It was the only answer I could give to avoid a bashing later. The disbelief on their faces wasn't lost on me, but my father beamed proudly at my learned response while my mother quickly downed a drink and got up to get another. Inside, I was crying, desperate to tell one of them the truth. After all, they were all parents. Surely not all the fathers here were getting it on with their daughters? Surely one of the women could see I was saying what was expected and not what I wanted to? Surely not all of them were as blind as my mother seemed to be?

But no, I got dragged around to drunken party after drunken party, and each night ended the same way: me driving my drunken parents home; my mother puking her guts out and saying she'd never drink again; my father being syrupy sweet to her as he tucked her into bed and kissed her goodnight...she was his little girl now... and then me, huddling in bed, listening, praying he wouldn't come into my room once he was sure she was asleep. But he always did. I woke up the morning after loathing life more today than yesterday while dad chatted on happily with my hungover mom about how drunk she'd been the night before. She remembered nothing about coming home. I remembered everything and to this day, I cannot stand the smell of whiskey breath.

What I have just shared with you, the drunken cunnilingus nights, has been one of the hardest parts for me to write. It is a time where my shame reached its peak, where I felt most depraved and utterly suicidal. I felt I couldn't sink much lower as a person and as a result had become what he said I was: ugly. What man would want me now? What man could look at me with any love or respect knowing I'd let my father do this to me, not once, not by accident, but repeatedly. What man would understand why I couldn't stand up for myself, why I didn't run away, why I didn't go to the police? No, I was what he had told me for years: ugly, stupid, unloveable. A whore. Only he could love someone like me. I should be grateful that at least he wanted me and could give me all the things other men could, and better!

Sometimes at home alone, depressed, crying tears neither my parents ever saw, I got close to taking a knife and plunging it into my belly, but I couldn't do it. The very fact that I lacked the courage to run away or commit suicide made me hate myself even more: I was gutless on top of everything else. How despicable I was! The more I thought about that, the more I bought into his reasoning:

"What would you gain by running away?" He asked me, knowing I didn't have a ready answer.

"How would you support yourself? Where would you go?" His face suggested how absurd the whole idea was.

And as he reasoned on, I thought yes, he was right. And then, what about mom? As much as she was virtually invisible in my life now because it was so dominated by him, how could I abandon her? Though we never talked about his utter control over my life and her insignificance in this "family", what would become of her if I left? Sometimes I'd almost convince myself that if I were gone, he'd begin having a normal sexual relationship with her again and all this would be over. But then I'd think, "I'm kidding myself ". He'd told me often enough, almost like a confidante in some nefarious scheme, that he only had sex with her now and then so she wouldn't become suspicious, that he didn't desire her at all. He'd say,

"If you left me now, how would I satisfy my needs? After all, wouldn't it look strange if I suddenly started having sex with mama 3-4 times a week? How would I explain it? You couldn't do that to me, could you love?"

I couldn't care less about how he'd satisfy his damn needs but when he talked like this, usually after sex on that fold-out while mom was still napping, because he was calm after getting his evening "naughty" as he called it, I didn't dare argue. The last thing I wanted was him getting angry. Peace at any price, remember.

It was on those evening, after-sex talks, that if he wasn't brainwashing me about how foolish it would be for me to tell anyone or to leave, that he manipulated my emotions yet another way. Now sexually satiated, my father the abuser would disappear and my dad, reappeared. He'd talk to me about life, world events, science & physics (which he loved), the war and what is was like living in the prison camps under Hitler. He'd even talk about the hopes and dreams he'd had for himself and mom after the war, how he hoped immigrating to Australia would mean freedom and happiness and a chance to become somebody. He also told me how devastated he was when news came to him that mom was having an affair back in Germany while he was slaving away, digging trenches under the hot Aussie sun, preparing for the arrival of his wife and child to their new home. And he told me, with tears in his eyes now, how mom had wanted to stay with her lover in Germany, keeping me, his only baby with her. Mom had broken his heart, just like his own mother had when she died from T.B. when he was only ten. He'd felt utterly abandoned when his mother died and he'd spent years looking for another woman to love. He'd found mom. And now she had deceived him and wanted to take away his little girl too. He would never let that happen. I was all he had then...and now. As I listened, I tried not to feel sorry for him, but somehow I did. He too had been hurt. Maybe that was why he was like this?

"And just as I'd never let them take you from me, as I'd never abandon you, I know you would never abandon me, would you? I know you," he said softly, lovingly. "You are a good woman, a loving daughter. You are not like your mother. You wouldn't deceive me. You will always be faithful to me, won't you?"

These weren't really questions. They were veiled demands, spoken softly, kindly but insistently, every one hitting where he intended, tying me to him, guilt- tripping me, manipulating me and also lulling me into a false sense of safety. As I'd listen, I'd feel his pain, his need, and I'd forget my own for a while. I'd sense how much this man, the nice one, really did love me and need me. Of course I couldn't deceive him as the other women he'd loved had done. I would hang in there. After all, the abuse couldn't go on forever, could it? Sooner or later, the nice dad would be grateful for my loyalty and realize it was time to let me go. He would do the right thing, wouldn't he?

And so my father managed to keep me trapped. I was a dragonfly, born with wings, but now so tangled in a sticky web of uncertainty, lies and confusion spun by my father that I could no longer fly.

DRAGONFLY

Trapped in a web of deceit
Snagged on threads of shame
Once violated, a child,
Like the dragonfly
Will never be the same

She cannot free herself
So she looks for help from you
And if you don't set her free
Then what else can she do?

You must believe her story
She has no reason to lie
But if you turn away from her truth
You leave her there to die

©*Viga Boland, June 2013*

CHAPTER 19: ADOLESCENT VIAGRA

One thing is certain about my father: he was very intelligent. He had both a sharp mind and a way with words, both of which made him, as is obvious from what I've written so far, a born manipulator. But if there's one thing he never seemed to grasp it's that you can't demand or force someone to love you. He'd tried that with mom and failed. She stayed with him because she lacked the inner strength to leave. She lacked the confidence needed to be independent and in charge of her own decisions and life. He demanded love from me too, but failed to see that loving someone is a personal choice and you can never love fully if you aren't given the choice in the first place or you've lost all trust in the person demanding the love. And when fear is added to the mix, love is interwoven with hate.

Just as my father believed he could force me to love him and that over time, I would find his definition of love easy and natural, the time came that he also felt I should be enjoying the sex he was forcing on me. He seemed puzzled that at 16, with a now fully developed woman's body and, he assumed, natural cravings for sex, that he couldn't get me to orgasm. Initially, his only interest was his personal satisfaction, but now, after years of unnatural and unwanted intimacy, he wanted all this to be "good" for me too. Ugh! My brain, my body, my innermost core fought him on this one: he'd given me no choice in the first place, but I did have the choice to not be a willing participant, to not to let him win this battle too. As I'd zone out and go somewhere else in my head, or be so focused on listening for mom, my body refused to relax and my mind wouldn't let it. Letting myself enjoy sex with my father would be the ultimate betrayal, and I would be both the betrayed and the betrayer. I refused to let that happen. I had to keep that one last shred of self-respect.

So when all his fingering of my clitoris, experimenting with different sexual positions and alternate verbal coaxings and threats that I relax and enjoy myself failed to make me climax, he bought home some pills guaranteed to make me reach the heights of ecstasy. I was absolutely terrified of these silver-coated bullets some guy at work had sold him for a dollar a pill. Remember, this was the mid 60's. That was a lot of money back then. I recoiled as my father told me what they would do for me. Could these magic bullets really strip me of my last hold over him? If they were as potent as he said, were they some mind-altering drug and would I then become an addict? I was as petrified at the idea that my own father might now turn me into some kind of junkie as I was by the thought I might actually reach orgasm with my own father. That last thought horrified me more than the first.

When I hesitated to take the pill he held out to me, his smiling reassurance that they were harmless turned into anger at my refusal to do what I was told. His face filled with rage and his mouth twitched as he transformed into Mr. Hyde. He was my father: how dare I disobey! Then he'd soften, pop a pill into his own mouth to prove it wasn't poison (remember the yeast incident as a child?) and instantly again demand I swallow it "pronto"! My tears were useless. I swallowed the pill, shaking with fear of what it might do to me, and so angry inside that I'd lost yet another battle to him.

Days passed. I felt nothing changing in me from his damned pills. Good! They weren't addictive. Better yet, I felt nothing more than I ever had as he went in and out, in and out. He'd turn me this way and that, telling me to try harder, insisting I relax and let myself go. Surely these expensive pills were doing something for me? He said they were making him enjoy it even more. Like I wanted to hear that, or I even cared? The last thing I wanted was for him to enjoy it more! Inwardly, for once, I was smiling, even laughing to myself: he hadn't won this time. He'd just wasted money. Score one for me at last!

CHAPTER 20: SO THIS IS THE REAL YOU MOM!

I have just been reading over the last several pages of what I've written and one thing jumps out at me: the absence of my mother in all of this. I'm not really sure why. Perhaps it's because these years of my life were so dictated and dominated by my father that Mom is just a shadowy figure in the background. Like an extra in a movie, she appears in a scene now and then, seen but unseen and just about never heard. When I think back, the only conversation I remember between the three of us as a family is what was on TV that night, or where to go for a Sunday drive, or who would have the next party, or who had the best car or the nicest house...mundane, ordinary, and for me, insignificant and boring stuff. Mom's opinion was never sought on any important issues. Correct that: if they were looking for a house, she always spoke up about what she liked and didn't, but when it came to making a decision, my father was always the final word. And when it came to me, Mom had no word at all. Her opinion wasn't wanted nor asked for and didn't matter anyway. So she remains in my memory of those years as a sad, quiet little woman who worked hard days on the line at Christies biscuits and took naps every evening, who only laughed at parties when she was drinking, and whom all other men, except my father, found charming and beautiful.

I came to see more of that charming, even flirtatious woman that was my mother when I began working at Christies Biscuits during summer vacations. With help from some of her supervisors, mom got me a job there when I was 16. I was very excited about this. Christies paid summer students very well. I had visions of finally having some real spending money instead of the $1 allowance my father gave both mom and me weekly. Yes, you read right. In his eyes we each needed no more than $1 a week since all our other needs were taken care of and we never went anywhere without him anyway. And when he kindly opened his wallet and handed us each our $1 bill, we each kissed him and thanked him profusely as if he had bestowed something wondrous on us. It was a weekly ritual and our groveling in front of him was what was expected by the master from his slaves.

I don't know whose idea it was for me to get good paying summer work but it was probably my father's. He said I was becoming too expensive. Loretto College tuition fees were going up yearly and we had to think of university still ahead. I was no longer working weekends at Loblaws since we'd moved so I wasn't earning my keep that way either. In my father's opinion, I was becoming fat and lazy too, so sweating out the hot summers inside a biscuit factory would "melt away the blubber".

Factory work, the people and the entire environment was an eye-opener for me. It was noisy, busy, rushed and ever in motion. Mom and I travelled back and forth together when we were on the same shifts and I began to know her a little better as both a person and a woman, even as a mother. During my first few days, she'd slip over to my department (packing) during her breaks to see how I was doing. I was doing terribly! I was all thumbs! The biscuits came down the line row on row so fast I couldn't keep up. I'd reach for a dozen to slide onto the rippled inner paper on a tray and biscuits would fly into the air and onto the floor. By the time I reached for another 12, the long row of 36 or so that I should have cleared were way down the line. It was awful! Sweat was pouring off me, the supervisor was yelling at me, the other packers were scowling at me and my face was cherry red with both heat and embarrassment. When mom dropped by, she'd see my frustration and step in, swiftly grabbing the dozens and sliding them expertly onto the papers. I was floored by her dexterity and speed. She completely amazed me. For the first time in my life I felt a profound respect and gratitude for this competent little woman who was just a shadow of this skilled person when she was around my father. It was a respect and awareness of my Mother that would grow considerably over the next few years as she covered for me in ways other than picking up my biscuits.

On my breaks, I'd slip over to mom's department (icing) to watch her work. What I saw amazed me even more about her. She worked with such ease and speed, feeding tall rows of biscuits into a dozen or so hoppers. The biscuits dropped swiftly in rows from the hoppers and went down the line for automatic icing. Mom, known as Julie, managed to always have all hoppers topped up, while she chatted and joked with other "fillers" as they were called, and flirted amiably with male supervisors and floor sweepers who always found a reason to stop by and visit Julie. It was obvious the men loved her and she thrived on their attention. She was confident, smiling and knew her value as a worker and a woman. And she was such a far cry from the woman I knew at home. This woman was someone I admired and looked up to. Why did she so diminish and vanish in my father's presence?

Mom, in her 20's in Australia

"Our lives begin to end the day we become silent about things that matter"

Martin Luther King

CHAPTER 21: THE SUMMER WIND

After a few weeks in the packing department, it became embarrassingly obvious that I was seriously missing my mom's skills on the biscuit line. Fortunately, my mom had so much respect amongst the uppers at Christies that I didn't get fired. Instead, they decided to give me a shot at being a machine operator. Initially, the very idea daunted me: machine operators were better paid and had a higher profile, but they had a bigger responsibility too: if a machine broke down, entire lines were stopped and production was halted. Delays in production were costly. Keeping on schedule was a priority. So machine operators had to be alert at all times. I was terrified at the prospect of missing something that could bring thousands of rows of biscuits to such a sudden halt that biscuits could be seen bunching up into mountains of waste at the top of the ever moving lines because my machine at the end of the line had abruptly stopped! And I did see that happen a few times.

But as it turned out, the bosses' faith in me was well placed: while I severely lacked dexterity and speed in picking up ever-moving rows of biscuits, I was good on the machines. And when the machines were running well...and it was my job to make sure they did...the job was easy. It even left me time to think, daydream a little, scribble poems on scraps of paper, and chat with the very friendly mechanics who always seemed to have a reason to stop by.

One of these, Asher, seemed to stop by a bit more often than the others. He was a head mechanic. I first noticed him one day when I sensed eyes on me several lines away. He was working on a machine, but I became aware that he was looking at me as much as he was looking at the machine he was repairing. He was older but good-looking and there was something rather smoldering in his gaze that sent a little rush through me. I tried to ignore him as mom and others had told me he was living with one of the most attractive, and most jealous supervisors in mom's division, Vera. Vera was very friendly with everyone and very nice to me since she liked mom. But the word was she was a viper if anyone got near her man: she'd claw their eyes out. So as far as I was concerned, Asher could give me all the smoldering looks and winks he liked but I would steer clear of him. He spelled trouble and it wasn't just Vera I was worried about.

But, sooner or later, something had to happen. One afternoon, I had just missed my bus for work and was panicking about being late when a gorgeous sky blue 1957 Thunderbird convertible pulled up in front of me. It was Asher. We were both on afternoon shift and headed to Christies.

"You're going to be late..." was all he said. I could almost see his smoldering eyes undressing me behind his dark sunglasses. "Get in!" He reached over and pushed open the door.

Accustomed as I was to always doing what an older man told me to do, I obeyed. I was simultaneously nervous and secretly thrilled. I knew this man found me attractive despite my father's constant brainwashing that I was ugly and no man but him would want me. Somehow I knew this man did want me. But what did he want me for? We didn't talk much on that short ride into work but he knew I was nervous and kept telling me to relax. He was just giving me a lift. But somehow I sensed this was actually the beginning of something I didn't really want to happen on one level, but was as curious as any teen would be on another. And I was right.

Now, this is the point in my story where I could digress and turn this into a steamy *"50 Shades of Gray"* fantasy fiction, but this is reality, not fiction. What is significant about the entrance of Asher into my life was how it ultimately made me feel even worse about myself. By the time it was over, I felt further cheapened, dirtier and even uglier than before. Once again I'd given in, to some degree, to an older man's sexual desires because I didn't have the courage or even know how to say No! My weakness made me hate myself. But then, I'd never had the option nor experience on how to behave otherwise.

I did have an affair of sorts with Asher...a summer romance for a naive, abused teen, a fling for an older and very smooth operator who knew how to say the right things to try to get to what he wanted: another bedroom conquest.

But he never fully succeeded with me. I couldn't quite go where he wanted me to, but no wonder Vera watched him with eagle eyes. As I learned, this was typical of him and typical, it seems, of factory life. The lines were always filled with gossip about who was doing it with whom. And yes, the rumor mill was rife with talk, but no proof of something going on between Asher and me. In the end, it wasn't fear of Vera that made me bring the affair to an end. It was the fear that somehow my father would find out. Nothing, absolutely nothing, terrified me more than that. I kept picturing his Mr. Hyde face spitting and swearing at me; I could see his huge hands bashing me around my head and ears as he'd done for far smaller infractions when I was a child; I could feel the kicks to my backside that were bound to come if he found out. I did eventually get all of those when I met my husband many years later, but Asher wasn't worth that risk.

I returned to my final year of high school with Asher's favorite song, *"The Summer Wind"* still playing in my head and the scent of his Old Spice cologne lingering around me, still telling myself, as Asher had tried to convince me so often, that what was happening was love. I so wanted to believe that, but deep inside I knew I was deceiving myself. This was just another dirty older man eager to have his way with a naive, gullible girl desperate for real love but far from desperate for sex!

CHAPTER 22:THE PILL

I'm not exactly sure at what age I went on the pill but I do remember my father's reaction to my doctor's decision to put me on it. I'd been suffering horrendously with my periods, throwing up, headaches, swollen painful, untouchable breasts...all the things that added to my already deep-seated hate of having been born female. Why, I asked myself, and that God who never answered, did I have to put up with this monthly agony on top of everything else to do with being female? The only good I could see in it was that for 4 - 5 days of the month my father didn't enter me. Mind you, when he couldn't have sex with me vaginally, if he needed it, I was forced to bring him to orgasm manually, or to my utter disgust, orally. Now that was something I really loathed. I'd watch his face once mom went for her nap, wishing, praying that this evening he wouldn't be in the mood, especially since I had my period. Most of the time, he'd say "forget it" and I'd breathe a sigh of relief that I knew he heard and didn't like.

But now and then he'd lift that blanket, unzip his fly and wordlessly point to his erection. If I hesitated, his eyes flared in anger and down I went. Ugh! My insides churned in revolt as he groaned and moaned with pleasure. He'd usually pull my head away just as he was about to explode and he'd finish himself off into some Kleenex for which I was grateful. That was how he'd avoided getting me pregnant all those years too, i.e. withdrawal. But once or twice he suggested he wanted to come in my mouth. Bile rose in my throat at the thought and panic would set in. As he approached climax I'd be covered in sweat from both the heat of being covered by the blanket in case mom suddenly walked in, and from the anxiety that this time he'd come in my mouth. Once or twice he didn't pull out and I gagged and choked on the acrid-tasting semen as I tried not to swallow it but had no other choice. After it was over, he asked me if it was really as bad as I made it seem. I wanted to ask him if he'd like me to catch it in a cup for him so he could drink it! But of course, I never had that kind of nerve.

But getting back now to my going on the pill. I was happy at the prospect of suffering less with my periods but my happiness was quickly diminished by my father's reaction to the news. He was ecstatic! Now he didn't have to withdraw at the critical moment. Now he didn't have to worry about getting me pregnant. Now my periods wouldn't last as long. And best of all, now he could fully enjoy sex by coming inside me. O happy day...for HIM! I died a little more inside as he rejoiced. Over the years I'd done everything I could to not be a "partner" as it were to his depravity. I'd resisted and fought his early attempts at entry by tightening up my insides and crying out in pain at very prod. I'd escaped into another world while he was pleasuring himself so I could block it all out mentally and feel nothing physically. I'd shut off my senses when he manipulated my vagina with his fingers or tongue trying to bring me to orgasm. I'd felt nothing from the magic bullet silver pills that he'd made me swallow. I had become a master of using my mind to control my body when it came to sexual stimulation because somewhere deep inside me I believed that as long as I resisted and wasn't being a willing partner, I was still a good person. And somehow I still foolishly believed that as long as he didn't come inside me, I was still a virgin as the act was never completed within my body. Now, going on the pill had removed my last hold on innocence. Now I too was guilty of his sin. I shot up another one hundred points on the ugly scale and sunk to a new low on self-respect.

CHAPTER 23: MORE STIMULATION NEEDED

"Come see the radio I'm making," urged my father. "I'll be in my workshop in the basement."

This wasn't a suggestion or request. This was a command spoken with a smile so mom wouldn't think anything of it. You see, to my father's frustration and my short-lived delight, some evenings mom just wasn't sleepy and refused the nap he tried to convince her to take. So, on those evenings, he'd go off to his workshop instead of watching TV and I was expected to follow a little time later, bringing him a coffee and myself for dessert. I hated it. I'd put it off as long as I could, then make his damn "cuppa" and, full of growing tension, I'd take it down to him. He'd be beaming with pleasure when I locked the workshop door, have a few sips, smoke a cigarette, then start pawing at me. I couldn't stand the combined smell of coffee and cigarettes...still hate it today. He'd make me straddle him and seemed to enjoy this kind of sex even more. It was sneakier, a "new position" too to make it even more exciting for him. He called it "our secret rendezvous". Yes, after five years of incestuous sex with his daughter he was craving more excitement. After he was done, he'd ask me if this was more exciting for me too. He just didn't get it! I hated it, all of it! Exciting? Try scared...revolted...wishing I were anywhere but in his workshop checking out his "radio"!

Then came the evening he decided I was getting "too wide" down there. I wasn't "tight" enough. Panic shot through me! Oh no! He wouldn't, would he? Surely he wouldn't attempt anal penetration! He saw the fear in my face. He heard my protests. He ignored the tears that began to stream down my face. His need was all that mattered.

He turned me around and made me get on my knees on the cold concrete basement floor. Wedged between the furnace and his workshop table, I began shaking in fear, anticipating the pain and every fiber of my being screaming for God to intercede, strike him dead, anything but this! Instead of the rod of God striking down the sinner, I felt my father's swollen, hard rod prodding, poking and finally gaining entry into my anus. I screamed in pain. He whispered angrily:

"Shut up for Christ's sake! You want her to hear you!"

You bet I did. He pushed again. I screamed again! He was furious with me, but withdrew, afraid mom would hear. He waited a few seconds, listening for her, and then resumed his assault, but no longer anally. When he was done, I got up rubbing my reddened knees, with my nose running from the crying and my anus on fire. I was afraid to look at him. His face was twisting, twitching in anger. I had displeased him.

"Was it really that bloody bad?" he hissed at me. "Did it really hurt that much?" He sounded incredulous at the very idea of pain.

"Yes," I nodded, keeping my eyes down. "It really was that bad."

"What a shame," he replied, calm now that his passion had abated. His grin was a smirk as he winked conspiratorially and said:

"It really felt good for me. So nice and tight!"

When he said that, I wanted to take the sharpie blade on his table and slash off that penis he was tucking back in his pants. I felt such rage welling up inside me, such frustration that I truly wanted to kill him...or myself. I felt so debased, so worthless. My feelings, my needs, my person were nothing. I was nothing. How many more years of being a nothing could I take?

CHAPTER 24: GRAD BLUES

By the time I was nearing high school graduation, the pattern of my life seemed to be set in stone: outside of going to school, working at Christies on summer vacations, and catering to my father's every need and demand at home, I had no life. Outside of school, I had no friends. Nor did I have any social life with people my age. I wasn't allowed to go to parties or do anything the other girls were doing. Back then, there were none of recreational facilities and after-school clubs or classes youngsters attend these days to help them develop social and other skills. And no way would my father fork out dollars for "frivolous" "money-wasting" classes in dance, gymnastics, music or sport. No, according to my father, I had everything I needed at home: food, shelter, TV for entertainment and a man for my womanly needs. Besides, the demands of my studies, especially as I planned to move on to university, left me little time for silly past-times and parties. That was for empty-headed females, not his daughter.

So when the nuns and student council were planning the big Graduation celebration, which included the grad dance at the gorgeous Boulevard Club on Toronto's lakeshore, I resigned myself sadly to not attending that part of my big day. I knew no boys to even ask to the dance anyway. But the Loretto nuns didn't buy into my lame excuses for why I wasn't going to attend the highlight of graduation.

"What do you mean you won't be attending the dance?" Sister Camelia probed. "We expect all the graduating ladies of Loretto to attend this evening. What is the problem?"

I felt my face beginning to flush. I didn't know what to say. I couldn't tell her that at 18 my father wouldn't allow me to attend. That sounded too preposterous. They all knew me as a friendly outgoing student who had no home issues. In five years at the school, no-one had ever asked me about my home life and of course, I had never told anyone either. Neither students nor teachers knew me at all. I'd hidden his secret very well. Give me straight A's for secrecy!

"Is it the cost, dear?" she persisted. "If so, we have a fund set up to help students in need."

"No...no..." I stammered, desperately wishing I could tell her the whole damn thing. I felt like a 5-year-old, afraid to tell the truth. "No...I...well I can't dance..." I lied, feeling utterly foolish and flushing a bit more. I wiped my sweating palms in my uniform. My heart was racing. Sister Camelia noticed my nervousness.

"What is it, dear? What's bothering you. I don't believe you don't want to come or that not being able to dance would stop you. You don't have to dance anyway!" She smiled encouragingly. "So what's the real reason? Don't you have a beau?"

It was my turn to smile. Beau? Such an antiquated word. I wondered if Sister Camelia had ever had a "beau". But since she suggested that as a reason, I decided to go with it and get this over and done with.

"Yes...I mean no...yes, that's the problem...I mean no, I don't have a beau. Can I go now? I'll be late for my next class."

Sister Camelia wasn't going to give up this quickly. "Don't worry about being late. I'll look after that. I might have a solution for you. My nephew, Stephen, recently broke up with his long-time girlfriend. He's been devastated by the split. So unhappy. No-one can cheer him up and we're all just a bit worried he might do something really silly. We've been trying to convince him he needs to get over it, look around at all the other lovely young ladies out there, and see there's more to life than his past girlfriend. We need him to come out of his room and start living again."

As Sister Camelia explained, I could feel a knot growing inside my stomach. Why was she telling me all this about someone in her family? Heck, I hadn't even considered nuns had family! I'd never thought they could be aunts or sisters to someone. They were just these black-garbed women who breezed down the Loretto College hallways, slammed the desks with a ruler when the room got noisy, and lived in a world far removed from ours, especially mine. They had one foot in heaven while I already had both feet in hell! What on earth could she want from me and what did I have to do with her nephew? She continued:

"You are just the person who could help our Stephen come out of his shell and start living again. You have such a vibrant personality."

I did? Was she sure she had the right girl? Me, vibrant? I couldn't imagine any more drab and uninteresting than myself. I felt my neck starting to prickle and my face flushing. Where was she going with this?

"You and Stephen could help each other: you need a date for the dance. He needs you to save his life."

Whoa! Hold on! This was rather dramatic. Surely she was kidding?

"I'd like to talk with Stephen and tell him I need him to help out one of our young ladies. I think if I put it this way, he's such a nice boy he'll want to help out, especially if he doesn't see it as me trying to set him up with a date or something like that. What do you say?"

What do I say? I was speechless. My face flushed; my neck prickled. All I could think of is how my father would react to the idea. He'd be incensed. How could I even tell him what she had in mind? He wouldn't let me go anywhere with any boy for any reason. How could I tell that to Sister Camelia now when she wanted me to help her nephew. Arrrrggh! I wanted to scream. She sat patiently awaiting my answer. My mind was in turmoil. I didn't know what to say. So I blurted out:

"What if Stephen takes one look at me and wants to vomit!"

Sister Camelia burst out laughing. "What a funny thing to say! Why would he do that? You're a lovely looking girl!" (I was?) "Actually what if it's you who takes one look at Stephen and wants to vomit?"

Oh dear! Was he that bad? She stopped chuckling and explained:

"Actually, Stephen isn't the most handsome boy on the street but he is one of the nicest ones you'll ever meet. He has bright red hair, lots of freckles and some rather severe acne around his chin."

Oh boy! The mental picture forming in my mind with this description wasn't helping my nerves at all. Not only was she trying to set me up but she was setting me up with a creepy looking guy! Well, after all, how suitable: two uglies together made sense. Sense or not, I just wanted to bolt from her office. It was becoming uncomfortably warm, stifling.

"So what do you say?" she asked sweetly and seriously again now. "Would you mind? You'd really be helping out someone desperately in need of your help right now. You'd be doing a very good thing and Our Lord would be very proud of you for saying yes."

Oh boy. Did she have to bring "Our Lord" into this too. Nothing like pulling out all stops. If she only knew how Our Lord was the last person or entity I was worried about pleasing. Of course I could never say that. All I could think about was how to suggest all this to my father.

Sister Camelia, hands folded in her lap the way nuns do it, lightly fingering her long brown rosary bead belt, patiently waited for me to reply.

"I'll...I"ll think about it," I stammered. "Can I go now please? I'm really late for class and Sister Scholastica will be annoyed and..."

I bolted from her office wishing I could run right out of the building and just keep on running. Why did my life have to be so complicated! Stephen needed help? I needed far more help! I was trapped in a secret world of my father's creation and couldn't see any way out of it, not now, not ever. Was this to be the pattern of my adult life i.e. forever facing situations or opportunities I couldn't accept and couldn't give honest explanations for turning down. At 18, I could no longer use the excuse "My father won't let me," without people thinking I was weird or needed to grow up. My father had turned me into some kind of frightened freak who was crying inside but couldn't speak.

So what happened, you ask. Well, I don't exactly remember the circumstances of bringing up Sister's suggestion with my father but I must have timed it right and put it across in such a way that he agreed to let Stephen take me to the dance. I think I put the accent on this being a special favor for one of the nuns and explained why this was so important to her. My father was always big into keeping up appearances to others of ours being a good, caring and nice family, so perhaps opposing the idea would have made us look bad.

As the night of the graduation dance drew near, my father made certain over and over that I knew how good it was of him to let me go, that I was asking a lot of him and testing his kindness and patience, and that if it wasn't for the special favor to the nuns, no way would I be going. I had to thank him over and over again, though inside I was seething with every thank you. The night before the dance, he took me sexually in that basement workshop of his and tried to make me "come" to make sure my own sexual urges in the presence of other males would be under control. He didn't succeed at making me come any more now than he ever did. I refused to give him that one last satisfaction. I was determined to hold on to some part of my "virginity" somehow.

I was a bundle of nerves when Stephen arrived to pick me up. We had talked once on the phone to arrange time and give him my address, but until I opened the door, neither of us quite knew what to expect. Dressed as he was in a black tux, he didn't look quite as unattractive as the mental image I had of him. His hair was indeed bright carrot ginger and his face was narrow, even effeminate, and yes, there were the signs of acne that his aunt had mentioned. But his smile was bright and genuine and his sad eyes seemed to light up at his first sight of me. He looked so relieved that I couldn't help but wonder what kind of creepy looking girl he had been expecting!

My father was right behind me as I opened the door, keen to get the first look at this male intruder into his tightly controlled world. I heard him stifle a laugh and noticed him smirking at Mom who huddled off to his side. I knew immediately what he was thinking: this was no competition for my heart. It was indeed my father who invited Stephen inside. Stephen entered, holding a little clear plastic box with a pretty rose corsage for me. After some minor chit chat, I removed the corsage, unsure of who to ask to pin it on. I knew tradition was the escort did the honors but I sensed it might be a bad move to let Stephen get that close to me with dad right there. I made some inane comment, especially after catching a slightly ugly twist in dad's fake smile, and asked Mom to help me with it. She knew what both my father and I were thinking and obliged.

As we were leaving, my father reminded us for the umpteenth time that I was to be home at midnight, not one or five minutes after. Midnight. Okay, we both got it. Dad watched us till our car turned the corner and I let out a huge sigh of relief. I could finally relax for a few hours and be a normal young adult out on a date. And for the first time in my life, my Father wouldn't be ten feet away watching and controlling my every move, every word, every smile in the presence of males in a social situation. I planned to enjoy every minute with this nice young man who was helping me far more, I thought, than I was helping him.

The evening was great. We got on well with each other, drank punch, laughed and chatted with all the other grads. We danced, keeping a suitable distance between our bodies as was expected by the nuns and would have been demanded by my father. As it neared midnight, I so didn't want the night to end. Neither did Stephen.

"Call your dad," he urged. "Ask if we can stay another half hour."

My friends coaxed along with him. "This is graduation, silly. Who goes home at midnight? What, are you going to turn into a pumpkin or something? Call your dad and tell him you want to stay longer!"

For Stephen and my friends, it was a no-brainer: I was 18, an adult, free to come and go as I pleased. They wouldn't understand that you don't tell my father what you want to do: he tells you what you're going to do! When I tried to get out of calling, saying I didn't have any change for the phone (pre-cell-phone era remember), someone put a quarter in my hand and said, "Now call!" With hands pushing me toward the booth, I reluctantly and nervously dialed the number. My father picked up on the first ring.

"YUP?" he shouted. The tone of his voice instantly terrified me. I broke a sweat. My skin prickled. My stomach tied a knot. Nausea welled up.

"H...hi daddy," I stammered, instantly a little girl again. "H-how a-are you?"

"What's up!" he bellowed into my ear. "Are you on the way home?"

I was tempted to lie and say we had a flat or something to buy some extra time but knew he wouldn't believe me. So I told the truth:

"Well, not quite. I...we were wondering if we could stay just a little longer? My...my friends are all st-staying and no-one's going home yet. We...we..."

He cut me off before I could finish. His voice was mean, hard. I could almost see his contorted face as he replied through clenched teeth:

"Haven't you pulled me enough? I give you a finger and you take a hand!" He shouted the oft-repeated phrase at me. "I am so good to you and this is how you treat me? You tell that pimple-faced ugly carrot-head to get you home by midnight or else!" He slammed the phone down.

My ears ringing, and my hands shaking, I stepped out of the booth so glad that no-one, especially Stephen had heard what he said. Miserable with embarrassment and filling with fear of what awaited me at home, I stammered:

"We...we have to go RIGHT NOW!"

I ran towards the doors trying to not see my friends' shocked faces. Stephen ran after me saying our goodbyes. He looked puzzled as he opened the car door. I didn't know what to say to him. As we drove off, he asked what he needed to know. All I could say was:

"I'm sorry...I can't explain. My father is a very strange man and when he says midnight, he means midnight."

When my father flung open the door on our arrival, he backed up what I had just told Stephen. He was livid. He didn't care how he sounded or how much he was embarrassing me in front of Stephen who had politely walked me to the door. There was no goodbye peck on the cheek, no niceties, no inviting Stephen inside for a tea or coffee and no thanks for bringing me safely home. All Stephen and I heard was:

"So this is how you treat your father! It's five minutes after 12. Did I not say midnight? When I say midnight, I mean midnight! Where is your respect?"

With that, he pushed me into the hallway and slammed the door in Stephen's face without a thank you or goodbye. I wanted to die. I could just imagine the confusion in Stephen's head as he walked back to the car. Our fairy-tale evening had ended with an angry bang.

My father watched Stephen through the sheers as he drove off, all the time cursing him.

"Who does he think he is, pimple-faced creep, thinking he could keep you out longer. Probably hoped he'd get his cock into into your pants! Ha! Thinks he's a big man!"

He raved on and on. I just stood there cringing, hating what he was saying, hating him. He had turned such a lovely evening into something so dirty, so unpleasant. My mother, finding some small strength deep inside her, and knowing a beating was imminent the way he was working himself up, spoke up weakly, trying to calm him down:

"Bogdan stop. She was only five minutes late..."

He chopped her off immediately as he came toward me. "Didn't I say midnight is midnight? Not five minutes after.... Not one minute after!" he shouted as his foot came up and kicked me hard in the backside. I jumped in pain. He screamed:

"Don't you move, you filthy cunt, when I'm talking to you! How dare you disrespect me like that in front of some hormone-overloaded boy with milk still under his nose!" He smashed his fist into my head, shouting:

"First you try my goodness by asking to go to this thing? Then you tell me some jerk is going to take you. Then you want to stay longer than I kindly allow! Who do you think you are? Who do you think I am...some weak excuse for a man who allows a woman to push him around and tell him what she wants to do?"

He raved on and on, turning on my mother who stood by helplessly watching. "Well, what are you looking at?" he spat at her. "Why don't you just go to bed!"

She again tried to intervene. "Why...why don't we all just go to bed? We...we are all tired. She...she's had a long day!"

My father's face reddened. "SHE's had a long day? What about ME?" he yelled. "Look how mad she's made me! How much she's upset me!" He stopped for a moment, and his tone softened.

"But you've had a long day too, mama. You go on. Get yourself to bed. This isn't any of your business anyway.

Go on my little woman. You go to bed," he coaxed.

He put his arm around her shoulders and led her gently toward their bedroom. I stood riveted to the spot, feeling the pain in my head and backside thumping as I watched him lead her away. I braced myself for what was sure to follow.

He returned about ten minutes later. I hadn't moved. I was too scared to move. As he came back into the room, he whispered:

"Get that stupid dress off. The party's over. $50 for a dress you wear once. What a waste of money! But I let you have it because I love you." His tone was quiet now, full of self-pity. "To think this is how you repay your papa... such disrespect. Go. Go and get changed and we'll talk some more."

As I hung the lovely white satin dress in the closet, I started to cry. He was feeling sorry for himself? He couldn't feel sorrier for himself than I did for me. I'd had a taste of freedom. I'd felt normal for just a few hours. I'd had fun with people my own age. But there was no fairy-tale ending. Cinderella changed back into her rags. I wanted to crawl into my bed and wished it would swallow me so he couldn't find me, but I knew he was waiting for me to come back out so we could "talk".

I re-emerged and found him where I knew I would: lying down on that despised fold-out chesterfield. The T.V. was on at low volume...all the better to disguise the sounds with, my dear. The big bad wolf was ready and waiting.

"Come..." he coaxed, smiling that smile I loathed. "Let me show you what a real man, not a boy, can do."

On a very personal level, that sad finish to what had been a happy and important evening for me, left me feeling desperate about my future. I felt so hopelessly trapped! I could see no way out of my situation with my father. He played my emotions like a guitar maker, one minute loosening the strings to check them out, then tightening and tightening to see how far he could go before they'd snap. He'd grant me little freedoms, tell me I was grown up now and could make my own decisions, play nice to get into my head and just when I thought I could trust him and I'd disclose my own needs and wants, he'd slam me with his truth: he was my father and I had to obey him.

It mattered nothing that I was now 19. How dare I oppose any ideas he had for me! What kind of ungrateful daughter was I? When it suited him to use the fact that he was my father and I was his daughter and as such, I had better respect his wishes and demands, he used it. Any hesitation to do what he asked brought on a volley of hurtful words aimed at guilt-tripping me for being ungrateful, a bad daughter. If he told me once, he told me a thousand times how ungrateful I was, how no good daughter would treat her father the way I do.

"Get out of my sight you ungrateful child!" he'd scream if I asked for some small freedom. "Who do you think you are!" he'd yell. "Someone important? Someone special that you should get special favors? You are NOTHING, you hear me? Nothing! Get out of my sight! You are not my daughter!"

Those words, "you are not my daughter" hurt the most. They hurt even more than being told I was nothing. All those years, everything he'd asked and forced me to do I had done because he was my father and I was trying so hard to be a good daughter. I had always hoped, and so often he let me believe, that if I did as I was told, sooner or later he would reward me by setting me free and releasing me to live my own life. In his gentler moments, when the father in him did indeed surface temporarily, he'd say as much:

"What, do you think I expect you to stay with me forever? Of course I don't. I know the time will come for you to go and after all, I am your father. I love you. I understand. Just trust me. That time isn't here yet. Trust your daddy. I know what is best for you."

And so I'd go on trusting, believing that one day this nightmare would come to an end, because he was my daddy. I may have been 19, but I was still just a scared 12-year-old ... experienced in sex and naive about life.

Why ever did you make me your child,
the object of your lust?
How could you take your own child's heart
and fill it with distrust?
With every thrust inside my body,
you double thrust my soul
Stripping me of my self-esteem
and leaving me less than whole

I was your own flesh and blood;
you were half my life
How is it that you blurred the lines
and turned me into your wife?
Wasn't mother good enough?
Couldn't you find another?
No, instead you had to choose your child
and destroy both me and mother.

And when I finally got away
like a lamb who had been slaughtered
You piled the guilt upon my shame
and said I was no daughter
Well, what on earth did you expect
when you stopped being dad?
When you died, my only tears
were for the father I never had.

©*Viga Boland, April 2012*

CHAPTER 25: HOW LOW CAN YOU GO?

It was somewhere around this time that mom took very ill just after we came back from one of their adult parties. We'd all gone to bed (mercifully with no despicable "munching" from my father for a change) when I heard his voice speaking loudly, urgently. I came awake, thinking mom must be vomiting again from over- indulging in alcohol, and was about to roll over back to sleep, when my father barged into my room and told me he was taking mom to the hospital. I flew out of bed pulling on clothes as fast as I could.

Mom was in dreadful pain as we tore into emergency. She had a ruptured appendix. I stood by helplessly, worried sick she might die. As she succumbed to the anaesthetic, hallucinating and mumbling sweetly about seeing the cigarette she was smoking going through the wall (yes, she was smoking right there in the surgery waiting room) I smiled lovingly at her, thinking how much I loved this silent, scared little woman who always hovered in the background of our lives. She'd never had enough courage to stand up fully to my father to defend herself or me, but I knew she cared more deeply for me than she'd ever say. And I felt so incredibly sorry for her! She too was a victim, a victim both innocent and utterly ignorant of the great deceit by her husband with her daughter. I felt so ashamed.

My father was laughing at her funny little hallucinations, making jokes, being "cheery" as he put it, impressing the nurses and doctors with his easygoing and friendly nature. "After all," he told them, "I have to keep my wife's mind off it so she's not scared."

"Such a nice man," I heard one of the nurses say to another.

Mom started slipping under. As she dozed off, my father leaned over, stroked her brow and said:

"That's right, my child. Go to sleep now, little one."

Oh, the irony! I stood there numb, wanting to cry. There was his "child" being wheeled into surgery. And there stood I, his wife(?), his mistress, by his side. It was all so damn wrong!

A few hours later, the doctors gave us the good news: mom would be fine but would have to stay in the hospital for a few days. I was super tired as we headed down the hallway to our bedrooms when suddenly my father stopped me as I entered my room.

"Our bed is meant for two. You don't need to sleep alone tonight."

I tensed and broke an immediate sweat. Oh no! Please tell me he wasn't going to suggest I sleep beside him in their bed while Mom lay in the hospital? How low could he go? I started to protest.

"Dad...no...I can't...it's not right... I..."

His lips twitched. He was getting angry. Fear rose in me and I felt the familiar nausea begin. I knew it was useless to argue. Wordlessly, my Father steered me toward their bedroom. As I got near mom's side of the bed and hesitated, I could sense his growing excitement, his anticipation.

"Take your clothes off. All of them. I've always wanted to sleep naked beside you. Hurry up!"

He turned on the light to watch me. Shame washed over me as I undressed. All I could think of was mom. Such a betrayal by him, by me. I felt so filthy. I climbed into the bed, catching an unwanted glimpse of his naked body with that fully erect penis just waiting and I wanted to puke. I pulled myself as close to the edge of the bed as I could get, somehow stupidly believing I might prevent the inevitable by turning my back on him. He turned off the light and I tensed further, trying not to move, wishing I could just vanish as he climbed into the bed. His huge arm came around me and dragged my backside toward him. He was inside me in a second. I closed my eyes and felt tears pour silently down my face. My heart was heavy with shame and self-loathing.

As he dozed off still inside me, his arm still over me reminding me there was no escape, I watched the sun rise on another horrible day in my life. The doctor had said Mom would probably be in hospital for several days. Would that mean I would have to sleep in her place, so completely take her spot in yet another way for several days? How could he so betray the woman he married? How could I look my mother in the face? Would she see my shame?

Would she feel my pain? Would she blame me? Indeed, was I to blame? How had I come to this? Why was I so weak? Why couldn't I stand up to him? Why didn't I just leave? What was wrong with me?

Mom's sudden hospital visit marked another turning point for me. The adolescent in me departed over those few nights and the adult was born. But the adult was sick, confused and crippled. She had sunk to a new low, dragged under by her own weakness and lack of courage. And she couldn't have hated herself more.

> Unlike the bee
> Broken in flight
> We can fly again
> And soar to heights
> We never reached before
> When we come out from under
>
> ©Viga Boland 2012

Photo © John C. Boland

PART 3: ADULTHOOD

CHAPTER 26: HIGHER LEARNING

It's almost ludicrous to call this stage of my life "adulthood". Here I was, a 19-year-old woman, starting University, and still feeling every bit like that 11-year-old pre-teen who vanished in the attic 8 years prior. My father now so dominated my every thought and action that I was someone he'd made. His thinking, his way of looking at people and the world around us overshadowed any thoughts of my own. I was close to incapable of making any major decisions for myself because I wasn't allowed to. Or if I did, it was impossible to make them without worrying he'd approve.

Even selecting my university courses was done in consultation with my Father. I had to take math because smart people take math. It was irrelevant if I liked it or felt I could handle it. Well, as it turned out, I couldn't handle it! I hated all the statistics stuff, and barely passed! Besides I was way too busy daydreaming about the handsome instructor teaching the course!

I took philosophy because I ran out of choices and because "smart people" took philosophy: it was "good exercise for the mind". The professor was old and boring and the books were painfully deep for a girl ... yes, I was still so much a young girl. Like a budding teenager suddenly set in a classroom of boys, I was more than moderately aware of all the males around me, especially after being cloistered in an all-girl convent school for the past 5 years and trapped in a home prison for 8 years. Even the unattractive guys looked good to me!

"Haven't we met somewhere before?"

I turned toward the deep male voice behind me, not recognizing the oldest pick-up line in the book. How could I? So naive.

"No...no..." I stammered, trying to sound confident, cool, while my heart raced. I recognized the dark haired, handsome Italian guy I'd caught looking at me over his shoulder several times in my philosophy class. "I...I don't think so."

We were standing in line in the cafeteria. My face was burning. I felt flushed, excited. Was he just being friendly? His companion, a nerdy-looking guy wearing thick glasses was grinning and poking him in the ribs. Was he laughing at me or wondering why Mr. Italian would bother with this ugly chick? It had to be the latter. Who could be interested in me? Hadn't my father told me for 8 years that I was too unattractive for men to bother with and only he thought I was beautiful enough to love?

Mr. Italian extended his hand. "I'm John. I think I've seen you in my philosophy class, haven't I? This is my buddy, Mike. Who are you? I'd like to get to know you better."

John's voice was smooth, confident, seductive. His eyes were dark and running over my body. There was something about me he liked. I felt weak, attracted and scared. I'd be an idiot to make friends with him or any male on campus. But I couldn't help myself. My father was miles away. He couldn't see me. I closed my mind to the image looming of his face contorted in rage and jealousy if he were to see me right this minute. To hell with it! I needed to start living and what my father didn't know didn't hurt either of us.

Mike, John and I started sitting together in philosophy class. Mike always made sure it was John beside me, not him. I'd start tingling at John's nearness, feeling his fluffy grey sweater brush my arm. Mike always seemed to be laughing, almost smirking at both of us, but he wasn't unkind, just more "amused". I suppose it was rather amusing to see a good-looking guy like John interested in a homely girl like me.

I began taking a little more care with what I wore daily, struggling to find something that looked good on me. The pickings were sparse. I raided mom's closet one morning and found a tight-fitting red knit dress. It fit like a glove, showing off my now ample curves. I couldn't do anything about my face. My father wouldn't let me wear any make-up. But when I took in the whole picture in the mirror, with that sexy red dress and high heels, I didn't mind the transformation. My father wouldn't have approved, but John certainly did.

"Holy!" he exclaimed when he spotted me in the cafeteria. "Where did you get that dress?" John let out a loud wolf-whistle and growled. I flushed with excitement and blushed as his eyes raced over my body, lingered on my breasts and re-focused on my face.

"And red lipstick too," he crooned with a faint hint of bemusement at the one bit of makeup I'd dared to apply. "Why don't you add some blue eye-shadow and mascara? Then you'd really look hot enough to kiss!"

He didn't have to convince me. I wanted HIM to kiss me. Before long I was applying full makeup once I arrived at Uni in the morning and furiously rushing to remove it before my father got home from work. I wasn't always successful.

"Are you wearing makeup?"

My father was peering intently at my face, his own face not a foot from mine. He had just arrived home minutes after I had and I hadn't quite managed to get it all off.

"No..." I stammered as tension shot through me. Damn the cheap makeup remover!

"You're lying, aren't you!" he raged. "What, do you think I'm stupid? There's something black at the edge of your eyes and your eyes look red!"

"I...I was rubbing at my eyes. I got something in them on the way home, some soot or dirt or something. So I was washing them hard because they were so irritated," I lied.

I felt like a 5-year-old caught with her fingers in the cookie jar. He looked at me in a way that told me he didn't believe a word, but miraculously he let it go. Maybe he was just too tired to brow-beat me for a change. It never occurred to me to simply stand up for myself, to say, "Look, I'm 19 years old. I can do what I want and don't need your permission!" In fact, when I think about it, I don't think I ever said that to him, not even when I was 20, 30, 40...not ever!

That first year of university was eye-opening for me. For the most part I was disinterested in all my classes and did only what I needed to to pass. My focus was on broadening my social skills, decreasing my obvious naivety about the opposite sex, and making the most of every moment away from my father. I began to see how normal men and women lived and interacted. How I envied the couples who walked arm in arm or embraced openly. I so wanted the happiness I could see in my girlfriends' eyes as their boyfriends gave them a lingering kiss when they headed off to different classes. And most of all I wanted their freedom, the freedom to be themselves, to make their own decisions and own mistakes.

"Don't you see, kitten, why daddy makes these decisions for you? Don't you see how I am trying to keep you from being hurt? From making mistakes you'll regret?" My father was in full lecture mode, still teaching me about life as he saw it.

"All those other men out there...those boys you see at university? They want only one thing from you: to get into your pants!"

On this occasion, my Father was clarifying why he wouldn't allow me to be a bridesmaid for a very close family friend. Diane had just left our home after formally announcing she and her boyfriend of two years were engaged. I was so thrilled that she'd asked me to be her bridesmaid and so devastated and embarrassed when my father, not I, turned her down. He told her:

"Viga will be too busy with university exams in June to set aside the time needed to be a good bridesmaid. You should should ask someone who can give your wedding the attention you deserve."

Diane had looked at me in disbelief. She had no idea how very much I would have loved to be her bridesmaid. Nor did I tell her the truth until after my Father had died and she'd been long divorced, remarried and divorced again! My father had certainly trained me to keep a secret.

As I ended my first year of university, nearly failing both French and math, I got passing grades in lying to my father, learning to smoke so I could fit in with the crowd, skipping classes to hang out with friends at "The Coop" and beginning to feel I wasn't quite as ugly as my father had led me to believe. While I never did get more than a brush on the lips from John, he was good for my ego and it didn't even hurt too much when he told me he'd had a girlfriend all along, a blonde hairdresser who wasn't at the university, and to whom he was going to propose in June.

When I asked him where I had fitted into his life all those months, he said:

"You were on trial. If you had passed my test of undying devotion to me alone, I might have dumped Cheri for you, but you failed."

I forget now how he "tested" me. It's irrelevant, but it was obvious he and my father shared a similar approach to women: women were useful and could be manipulated.

"You were also my trial of myself," John elaborated smugly. "Through you, I could test just how much I loved Cheri!"

"So, what kind of marks did you give yourself?" I asked hotly, hurting at again having been used by a man.

"Oh, I passed with flying colors. I was able to resist you! As good-looking as you are, I realized I really loved Cheri and now she will be my wife."

With that John closed the door on our "romance", but hearing he considered me "good-looking" was reassuring as was knowing he had found me useful for something besides sex. At least he hadn't tried to get into my pants. Only my Father did that.

CHAPTER 27: THE COLLECTOR'S LOLITA

Despite everything, John, Mike and I remained friends until the end of term. One sunny afternoon, we emerged from the darkness of an old university building, busily discussing our answers to the questions on the philosophy exam we had just written. Slightly blinded by the sudden brilliant sunlight, I was so intent on arguing whose answer was right, that I almost didn't recognize the familiar figure of the slightly greying older man with his hands behind his back, casually strolling not fifty feet ahead of us. As he turned his head to the left, about to look over his shoulder, I recognized his profile and my heart leapt into my mouth! It was my father! What the hell was he doing here on campus? Spying on me?

My fear and panic instantly replaced my disgust. I broke away from the two men and started walking rapidly in another direction without a word of explanation. They called after me, but I ignored them. My father heard them as they were now close behind him in their hurry to get to their next class. Thankfully, by the time he spotted me off to their right, he didn't connect them with me. I took some deep breaths to calm my rapidly beating heart, swallowed my panic and flashed a false, surprised smile at my father.

"Wow! Er...what are you doing here, daddy?" I asked as if he'd just given me a most delightful present. I'd become quite the actress over the past eight years.

"Oh, I finished work early today because of another migraine, so I thought I'd come and pick you up. Save the bus fare, and you could get home sooner."

He put his arm around me like a boyfriend would and drew me close as if to kiss me. I cringed, mortified at the thought that my friends might see us. I turned my face sideways quickly so he got my cheek instead.

"What's up?" he demanded. "No kiss for Daddy?"

I was in turmoil, horrified, embarrassed and scared all at once. No-one, not a soul, knew about my situation with my father, and I wasn't ready to explain why a greying older man would be so familiar with me in a public location like this. At the same time, knowing how quickly his temper could flare, the last thing I needed was a scene right here and now.

"Of course I have kisses for you, daddy," I lied, stumbling over words I loathed saying. "I...I just don't think campus is the right place for it. Pe... people don't ki... kiss here."

Mercifully, he let me go, but still reached for my hand so we could walk toward the car the way couples do. I so wanted to die! But needing to defuse any possible blast, instead I asked:

"So...so how did you find me? The cam...campus is huge but you came to the exact place!"

He touched the side of his temple, winked and grinned that hated smirk.

"I'm just smart!" he bragged. He tapped his temple again. "Remember, I'm God. I know everything. I just wanted to see where my little girl spends her day."

He'd mutated into daddy again. "You know, I never had the good luck to go to University. I always wanted to. I love learning. I wanted to get the feel of being a student, going to classes, having deep discussions with other brilliant minds. That's why I like to talk with you. You have a bright mind, unlike your mom. You know, she never got past grade 4. She can't think deeply. I need a smarter woman with a good brain."

I let him ramble on while my heart returned to normal and my mind went elsewhere. All I could think of was would he try this again? I didn't believe his explanation for one minute. He had come to spy on me. He wanted to be sure I was being true to him, not hanging around with the males on campus.

And what would he have done if he'd seen me chatting amiably with John and Mike? I knew him well enough to know he would have reacted with controlled rage till he got me alone. And then? Even though what he would have seen was totally innocent...three students discussing a philosophy exam...he would have turned it into something else, so deep was his jealousy, so strong was his possessiveness. And so huge was my own fear of both him and of others who might discover the secret, that I promised myself to never walk out of class with males again. I simply couldn't risk it. My Father had just re-bolted the chains around the small sense of freedom I had been enjoying. Would I ever be free?

As I worked through my second year of university, I felt more trapped and isolated from normal life than ever. I'd finally resigned myself to the fact that I would never have the kind of life and love other young women enjoyed. My friends had boyfriends: they were looking forward to becoming engaged, and dated on weekends while I spent weekend after weekend at home watching TV with my parents for hours, wanting to scream from boredom.

My father would wait for mom to finally go to bed, and after she moved out from under the blanket on that despised fold-out chesterfield, I was expected to take her spot so he could have his way with me once he was sure she was asleep. This meant sitting through one late show after another, with him nudging me awake if he saw me dozing off. He loved watching the movie, "Lolita" which always seemed to be on the late, late show. He used it to point out how natural it was for a young woman to be with an older man. I was his "Lolita". Had he been able to read my mind, he'd have known I felt more like that poor girl in the movie, "The Collector", trapped and mounted on the wall like a butterfly for only him to enjoy.

Sundays were a drag. We always went for a Sunday ride, stopping for a snack, or if my Father was feeling generous, a full lunch at some diner. Occasionally, we'd look at model homes or visit open houses. My father was already planning that when I graduated and got a job, we'd move into something bigger and nicer in a better neighborhood. If there was one thing he and all their friends valued, after the hunger and poverty of the wartime labour camps, it was material possessions: good cars and good homes were more important than anything else. And my father's need for one-upmanship was greater than everyone else's: his daughter was at university; their children barely passed high school; his car, though second-hand, was the best model; our furniture was nicer than everyone else's; and when they finally found a new home, it would be the biggest and best of their friends' homes.

With that in mind, all money went into savings. At 20 years of age, my father increased my and my mother's "allowances" from $1 to $2, and together we thanked him profusely for his kindness. I don't know what mom thought as he bestowed his generosity on us, given the poor woman still worked uncomplainingly day after day at Christies Biscuits and brought home a weekly pay-cheque which she immediately handed over to him, but I was filled with enough disgust for both of us.

At the same time I loathed myself more and more: I was a falsehood, a big fat lie! It wasn't just the deception I was living under daily that made me hate myself: I hated the phony front I had to present even to him, ever pretending I was happy, always confirming that I loved him because he so demanded it. And as he guilt-tripped me more and more with the promise that I'd stay with him forever because he'd die without me, I'd lost all respect for myself. He'd told me often enough that I was ugly. Yes, he was right: even in my own eyes I was indeed, ugly.

Given how completely trapped I now felt, I threw myself a little more heartily into my studies during my second year. At least I got away from my prison for hours during the day and could always use the excuse of so much work to do in the evenings that I couldn't spare the time watching TV re-runs night after night. Mercifully, my father understood that. After all, it was important to him that I get that B.A. It was a feather in his cap to have a daughter with a degree. I couldn't care less but I was also sensible enough to know that if I wanted to get a good-paying job, a degree would help.

I had no clear idea of what I wanted as a career because, again, I had so little to go on with my lack of knowledge of life beyond my home. And ultimately, I knew the decision wouldn't be mine anyway: it would be my father's. I'd always wanted to be an airline hostess. My father shared my fascination with flying, but no daughter of his would become a mere sky-high waitress! No, she would be a scientist or engineer. But he also recognized I had no interest in those professions. So it was easy to settle on that most desirable and usual one for women: teaching. I selected English as my major and ploughed through Chaucer and all the other boring old English writers. Even that was more stimulating than my home life.

Since little was to be gained by hanging with my friends smoking and drinking coffee at The Coop, I began to spend lots of time at the University library, researching and writing essays. I was lost in thought one day, when a male voice interrupted me:

"Do you mind if I sit here, opposite you? There are no other chairs available."

Startled, I looked up at a smiling, mature, slightly older student with friendly eyes and a twinkling silver tooth. I liked him immediately.

"By all means!" I replied, perhaps a little too enthusiastically.

Martin was German and had just moved here temporarily to finish his Masters degree in French and Italian. He spoke fluent English and had a charming European air about him. He wasn't especially handsome, but he was well groomed and well-mannered. I couldn't help but think that had my father been a normal father, he would have approved of Martin: bright, friendly, intellectual but not boring.

Over the year, Martin frequently joined me in the library. We'd chat about classes, assignments and essays. There was nothing romantic about our friendship though I secretly wished it could evolve into something. He'd chuckle, but not unkindly, at my general naivety. There was something comforting about him. I found myself wanting, on more than one occasion, to open up to him, to tell him about my hideous secret, but I held back. I was too afraid that if I did, he'd be utterly repulsed by me and I needed a friend. So I said nothing.

Toward the end of the year, Martin introduced me to a couple of his classmates who often accompanied him to the library. Tony and Rico were both 3rd year Masters students. I felt somewhat intimidated and stupid around these three "Masters", when I was just in a general B.A. course. They were always discussing heavy topics, while I was a bit like a giddy teen filled with girlishness in the presence of intelligent men. But none of them was ever condescending: they just made me feel better about myself than my father ever could or would.

As the year ended, Martin informed me he was leaving University of Toronto to complete his final year at Western U in London, Ontario. I couldn't believe how disappointed I felt. I realized then how much I'd come to care for him though nothing had ever been more than friendly between us. He had made me laugh, had made me feel good. He'd taught me some German, told me about Europe. He'd even visited my parents' homeland, Poland. He was worldly. I wanted to go with him. I dreamed of transferring to Western but deep in my heart I knew it would never happen. And when he told me he and his fiancée were getting married as well that summer, I flushed with embarrassment that I'm positive he noticed but was too much of a gentleman to mention. He had never told me he was engaged but then he'd never really given me any reason to think of him as anything but a friend. My own naivety, my own need had made him something so much more to me.

"I'm leaving you in the good hands of Tony and Rico," Martin told me smiling his wonderful big grin, his silver tooth twinkling away.

"I told them both to look after you because you are special and need their guidance and friendship."

Martin winked at me then and some unspoken understanding passed between us. Did he know? Had I inadvertently let something slip about my Father? Had he somehow seen through the brave, confident mask I wore daily to the frightened little teen behind it? I felt sure he had and loved him more for seeing the real me but never mentioning it.

CHAPTER 28: HAPPY NEW YEAR

Time out! Today, as I write this, it is December 31, 2012. A new year is about to begin. I have been re-reading sections of this memoir, wondering if I've left out something worth telling and wondering why New Year's Eve has never excited me as it does so many others.

My younger daughter has just gotten off the net after staying up all night to send kisses and best wishes to her boyfriend in Australia who went home for Christmas. She misses him horribly right now. After all, lovers love to see in the new year together. There's an old belief I've heard bandied around over the years that those with whom you spend New Year's Eve are those with whom you will spend the coming year. And the belief goes on to say what happens on that eve portends what will happen over the coming year. Now, just like I don't put much faith in religion, I don't hold out much for old beliefs either, except for one thing: this one day of the year always makes me feel a bit blue. Why? The answer probably rests in the New Year's Eve that preceded my final university year.

My parents and all their adult friends had tickets for dinner and dancing at one of the Toronto Polish halls. As I had no social life outside of their lives, I accompanied them. None of the other children in the families came along. They were all at parties with friends their own age, the parties I was never allowed to attend. Mom and I dressed up nicely and looked good, like sisters more than like mother and daughter. She looked so pretty I felt ugly and awkward beside her. I secretly hoped my Father might agree and forget about me for once.

As the music and dancing started, as was expected of the men, my father asked mom for the first dance. He immediately came to me for the next dance. As we finished, a good-looking young man approached my father and me, and with a slight bow, extended a handshake to my father and asked for the honor of dancing with his daughter. This was how it was done back then, a sign of respect.

I was a mixture of excitement and dread, expecting my father to refuse, but he didn't. The handsome young man led me onto the floor and I couldn't believe I was in the arms of a young male, a complete stranger, while my father was watching. And watch he did. I kept glancing anxiously at my father, so much so that the young man noticed.

"Why do you keep looking at your father?"

I didn't know what to say. How do you tell a stranger that your father doesn't allow you to date, gets insanely jealous, and has sex with you instead of his wife? I brushed off his question, laughing,

" ... nothing worth talking about."

As soon as the dance finished, in a most gentlemanly manner the young man returned me to our table. Again with a slight bow, he asked my father:

"Sir, may I have permission to dance with your lovely daughter again later?"

I tensed up, wondering what my father would say. I expected him to refuse but how could he? All his friends were watching and listening for his reply. It was as if he was being tested and he had to keep face.

"Since you ask so politely, yes, you have my permission."

I tried not too exhale too loudly in relief. I couldn't believe my ears. Several dances followed and I began to relax and really enjoy the night and the attention of my young partner. At last, my father was allowing me to be a normal teen, in public yet! It felt wonderful. Perhaps my life was finally about to change. Maybe the new year would be a great year for me! I was filled with excitement and hope.

As the clock approached midnight, I felt a growing trepidation. I'd caught my father's angry twitch a couple of times when the young man continued to ask me to dance, and I almost hoped I would be dancing with my father when the clock struck 12. I knew my father would expect the first kiss I'd give anyone would be to him. But the countdown started in the middle of a dance with my young partner, and before I knew what was happening, he was kissing me full on the mouth. Out of the corner of my eye, I could see my father exchanging quick kisses with my mom and friends, but he kept glancing toward me as the music drew to a close. The young man escorted me back to the table, extended his hand to my father to wish him the best. My father's handshake was quick and dismissive. Then he turned furious eyes on me as he hissed in my ear,

"Whore! You filthy stinking whore! How dare you let that hot in the pants punk kiss you! You slut! I'll speak with you later, you disgusting whore! How dare you shame me in front of our friends by acting like a slut? Whore!"

I died inside. I flushed with embarrassment and fear. All the Polish friends were talking quietly, pretending not to notice, but they knew he was angry, even if they didn't fully understand why. They had noticed his hand coming up ready to strike me, but suddenly he'd held it back, saving it for later. My father grabbed his jacket and told mother it was time to go. His face was red with curbed rage. Mom was feeling no pain after several hours of drinking.

"But Oleg just got me another drink," she protested cheerily.

"Oh, sit down Bogdan!" urged another friend trying to defuse the situation. "The night is still young. Relax. They don't close for another hour! Have another drink!"

My father sat down but his face wouldn't stop its angry twitching. I was terrified of what I knew lay ahead. I sat there frozen, shaking, scared. When I saw the young man coming toward us for another dance, I didn't need to look at my father to know that accepting would be madness. I politely turned him down, saying I was tired and sleepy. He looked confused but walked away. I glanced at my father. He nodded approvingly and patted his knee. That meant I should sit on it. I did as expected and felt so stupid, so childish as he put his arms around me and let everyone know I was his alone. I caught the puzzlement on the young man's face as he looked our way and I cringed inside.

My father, calm again now, chatted amicably with everyone. I started to relax. Hopefully, the worst was over. I watched longingly after the young man as he was leaving, but he never looked back at me.

After the hall closed, my parents invited everyone back to our place for a nightcap. They all came, I believe as much to try to keep my father calm as for a nightcap. But, as could be expected, one drink led to more and suddenly the room erupted in argument as someone questioned my father's anger back at the hall.

"Why did you get so mad, Bogdan, when that nice young man gave Viga a friendly New Year's kiss?"

"What's the harm in exchanging kisses on New Years Bob? Everyone does it. And after all, Viga is a grown woman!"

"Why was Viga even with us oldies? Why wasn't she out with friends her own age?"

My father exploded! I had shamed him!

"The first greeting of the year should have been for her parents, not some jerk she'd just met!"

"Yes, but the clock sounded in the middle of her dance," someone argued. "What was she supposed to do? Run over to us?"

"She knows bloody well what she was expected to do!" my father responded hotly. "She is a disgrace, an ungrateful daughter! She was nothing better than a street whore, dancing with him all night, throwing herself at him and then letting him kiss her full on the mouth like that. She was nothing but a piece of cheap shit!"

Some of the women in the room jumped, startled by the vehemence of his reply. The men shook their heads in silent disbelief. I sat there wanting to die, trying to stifle the tears that had begun rolling down my cheeks. Seeing my tears, one of the dearest friends who always listened first and spoke last as he absorbed all details, tried again to defuse my father's unnatural anger:

"Bogdan, she didn't act shamefully at all," said Frank calmly. "She was just a young girl enjoying herself. She has every right to dance with a young man and even be kissed by one at her age. You are acting as if she'd gone off somewhere and had sex with him. To be honest, your reactions are more like those of a jealous lover than a father! If I didn't know better, I wouldn't know what to think of YOU, not her!"

Frank had chosen the right words to say to my father who knew he had come dangerously close to being "busted" as it were, amongst his friends. And for my father, "keeping face" was paramount. He started laughing, pretending it was all a big joke:

"Aw...I'm just having fun with her," His false laugh

sounded hollow but he persisted.

"Just reminding her what her mama and I expect of her, right mama?" He glanced over at mama and winked, as if her opinion mattered. She and I knew it didn't, but she helped him keep face.

"Right," she slurred, raising her plastic cup of whiskey to him. "Papa's always right!" And she downed the glass in one gulp. He continued:

"We've always taught her to be a lady and respect herself so young men like that don't get the wrong impression."

He blathered on, lying to save face. I doubt anyone believed him. I certainly didn't. My fear rose as they left. I knew the worse was yet to come. As he closed the door behind them, he turned to my mother.

"Go to bed, mama. It's been a long night and you've had too much to drink. We'll clean up. And she and I have some talking to do, don't we?" he said, looking at me threateningly. I could see Mr. Hyde was impatiently waiting just below the surface, eager to rip into me. Before mom pulled the covers over her head, his huge fists were already pummeling my face, head and ears, and as the sun rose on a new year, every thrust of his hated penis drove home the point that I was his and his alone.

Happy New Year darling.

CHAPTER 29: WILL YOU MARRY ME?

The new year had gotten off to a nasty start and I couldn't wait for the new semester to begin so I could get away from home during the day. Martin had left for Western university in London. I felt isolated again, but true to Martin's prediction, Tony and Rico stepped in to keep an eye on me. Of the two, Tony was the good-looking one, but he was already taken. His fiancée, Gina, often joined us for lunch at the Coop, and it was exciting to hear her planning their wedding which was to take place shortly after graduation.

I don't really know when it suddenly dawned on me that of the two men, it was Rico who had become my constant companion. He always seemed to find me in the library, was the first to notice when I entered The Coop, and always found a chair for me at their table. He was a tall, slim Italian. He reminded me of Bill way back at Loblaws, the one with the Buddy Holly look, right down to the black horn-rimmed glasses and hairstyle. He was highly intelligent, impeccably dressed in suit and tie daily, and utterly polite and well-mannered, a true gentleman who opened doors for ladies, gave up his seat on the bus, and stood up when a lady got up to leave the table or a room. Next to him, I felt "common", unladylike, uneducated, uncouth, and given my personal life, unworthy of his attentions.

Perhaps it was my very "commonness" that drew him to me like a lovely innocent moth to a flame. Socially, he was so far above me, yet I sensed I had some kind of power over him that I didn't myself recognize then: my sensuality. He was a needy virgin, a virgin who was falling hopelessly in love with the wrong person. He really wasn't my type. I just didn't know how to refuse his advances without hurting him, so I went along with what he seemed to need from me.

I suppose we were an amusing sight for the janitor who always seemed to be cleaning the stairs at the exact time we'd begin a furtive form of fully clothed sex in the stairwell of one of the newer buildings. Rico always stood with his back to the stairs, hiding me and his obvious arousal as he pressed himself against me, trying desperately to control his body movement as he climaxed in his clothes, throwing his head back in an ecstasy I didn't share. I'd watch him, almost detached, intrigued by how I could have this effect on a man. I loved him as a friend but felt no attraction to him otherwise. I couldn't help how he felt about me, but I couldn't return his feelings. And because he was my friend, I felt guilty for letting him get his sexual release with me this way. It wasn't right to let him think it could ever be more than this, but I didn't know how to tell him that.

So when one day after a stairwell session, as he lit cigarettes for us both and placed one playfully between my lips, and asked me:

"How would you like to see Rome and Venice?"

I didn't think of his questions as anything more than his telling me again about his beloved Italy. But he went on:

"I think it's time I introduce you to my family. My mama is dying to meet you. I've told her all about you. She can't wait to see if you like her spaghetti bolognaise and tiramisu."

Before I had started to grasp what he was suggesting and could protest, he grinned and said:

"My papa too is very curious about this non-Italian girl who he thinks is spinning his son's head around." Rico smiled and squeezed my hand lovingly.

"Mama said to papa the other night that this girl must be very special when there were so many nice Italian girls in our community who would love to have her Rico's heart. But I told them both that no Italian girls I know are as nice as you!"

Rico kissed me lightly on the forehead then and told he was planning to book an appointment for us with a photographer within walking distance from the university.

"We can go on one of our lunch-hours and I'll pay for everything. I want a picture of you to show mama and papa and for me to look at every night before bed."

Now my head was spinning. I was speechless at what I was hearing. What was all this about and where was it heading? What on earth did Rico have in mind? We were just friends after all, university corridor "playmates".

I went along with the photo session and hated the results. I hated the girl in the pictures: she was ugly, a gutless, soiled phony. Rico loved the photos. His mama said the girl was "Si Bella!" His papa told his son he had a good eye for a beautiful woman. Beautiful? Me beautiful?

"And they both keep asking me when you are coming for dinner!"

I kept frantically trying to avoid the subject or come up with a suitable explanation for why it wasn't possible. The fact that Rico didn't have a car and that we lived at opposite ends of Toronto helped. But how much longer could I stall without telling him the truth?

I realized the depth of Rico's feelings when he began riding the streetcar home with me just to have more time with me than stolen moments in the stairwell or chatting with the group over lunch at the Coop. Doing this was completely out of his way and added two hours to his day just riding the streetcar to the end of the line, then returning in it to the city to go to his own home. He was in his 4th year of his Masters degree and would be graduating soon. His workload was huge. This unrequited "love" was affecting his studies.

Our relationship was also making me very nervous. Between the pressure to meet his parents and the increasing pressure imposed by my lack of freedom at home, coupled with the fact that I knew he loved me but I didn't love him, I knew I needed to end it all but didn't know how. It would mean hurting someone I didn't love but who was dear to me.

As the college year drew to a close for the summer, Rico gave me the "out" I needed. It was a brutal moment of realization for me from which I came away hating myself more than ever.

"So, what do you think? Rome or Paris this summer?" Rico teased as we walked toward our last classes of the day.

"Ha ha!" I laughed. "How about my backyard or Sunnyside Pool on the Lakeshore when I finish my shifts at Christies!"

I was still working my way through University at the biscuit factory over summer vacations. "Paris? Rome?

Dream on! I don't have money for that kind of holiday!"

Oh, but I do!" Rico replied, his face beaming, proud, full of anticipation. "I have lots of money. With me, you will never have to worry about money. So, don't you think it's a good idea? Which would you prefer for our honeymoon? Or we could do both if you want?"

I was floored! Speechless!

"Honeymoon?" I stammered. "H...honey...I...I... you're not serious, are you?"

"Why not?" he asked brightly. "I think it's a wonderful idea! You know how I care about you. I think we'd be great together!" He stopped, seeing my face in shock.

"Oh, I know...you didn't realize I'd want this so soon but with graduation coming, I'll be looking for a placement come September so it's logical we honeymoon in the summer, don't you agree?"

We'd reached our classes and I bolted into my room with a hurried goodbye, grateful to be able to get out of this awkward conversation so I'd have time to think of an answer as to why NO, I didn't agree at all and NO, I didn't think any of it was a good idea. Surely he wasn't serious!

But he was, and the critical moment of decision and honesty came soon after. I've never forgotten it.

My father had let me start driving his big gold-colored 98 Olds to University. I was showing the car to Rico late one afternoon before heading home when he asked to sit inside it with me. After admiring its flashy interior and the usual talk about cars, he steered the conversation to what was uppermost on his mind and what I'd been desperately trying to avoid: us.

"So...!" he started forcefully, "now that you're driving there's no more reason you can't come to dinner at my place and finally meet the family, is there?"

It was a statement, a foregone conclusion. In his mind, any objection would be over-ruled. "After all, if we are going to be married, it's time to start making some plans."

My skin started to crawl, my face flushing with rising blood pressure as I scrambled for excuses or reasons for why this marriage talk could go no further. I couldn't tell him about my father...couldn't and wouldn't...and I had no idea how to tell him I didn't share his vision of our future together.

I sat there squirming both mentally and physically as he chatted on happily about how, when, and where the wedding should take place. I was so overwhelmed I began zoning out as I'd done for the past nine years or so with my father. Once again, a man was telling me, albeit gently and sweetly, what he thought should be done, what he saw as best for him. But what about me? Did my thoughts, wants, needs matter?

"Hey...are you listening?" Rico's soft voice suddenly invaded my inner turmoil. He had turned to me in the car seat and was holding something in his hand. His face was full of emotion, his eyes hopeful, imploring, as he handed me a little ring box and urged me to open it.

"Will you marry me?"

Those four little words so many women dream of hearing shot an arrow through my brain! I'd reached a point of no return: it was time for truth. My whole life so far was a big lie. I didn't know how to tell the truth. And now I was looking at a sparkling diamond ring I couldn't accept and was about to break a person's heart.

"Oh, Rico ... I ... I don't know what to say..."

"Say yes!" he urged. "Please say yes! You mean the world to me. I want to be with you forever, take you to see places you've never seen, make babies with you! Please tell me you want the same things as I do! I know we would have a wonderful life together."

"No! No!" I blurted. "No...we cannot have a wonderful life... or any kind of life together, Rico...it's just not possible!"

I couldn't look at Rico, couldn't bear to see the pain I knew would be in his face. I just kept staring at the pretty ring in its box.

"What is it?" he asked. "Tell me! Look at me! Do you not love me enough to marry me? I've been patient. I haven't demanded. I understood you holding off meeting my parents, but it's time. Look at me! Please...what is it?"

I looked at him, saw the despair and hurt in his face, and began to shake. I couldn't say the words he was desperate to hear. They would be a lie and it was time for honesty, or as close to it as I could get. I closed the pretty little box and handed it back to him, and given how much I was shaking, said as calmly as I could:

"Rico ... I can't marry you. I can't marry anyone. You don't really know me but I can't talk about it. I care for you deeply, but...but..." I struggled for a way to say it without hurting but couldn't find it. "But I'm not in love with you."

I could almost feel those words slapping Rico's face and tearing into his heart. He so didn't deserve to hear them and I honestly never thought I'd have to say them to him. Worse yet, though he didn't know it, they were only part of the reason for rejecting his proposal.

"I don't understand..." he started, his face etched in pain and his voice breaking with emotion.

"All these months...all that's passed between us. Me talking to you about traveling in Italy, meeting my parents! Surely you knew how I felt? How could you let me believe you felt the same way? What was this for you? Just a game?"

Rico began to cry. I felt so horrible, vile. What kind of human being had I become? Was I heartless? Is this what my father had turned me into: an emotionless woman who ignored the feelings of others just as he did mine? Or had I so closed off my heart to other men for fear that I might just truly fall in love and have to face my father to fulfill my own needs and wants? Yes ... that was it: it was easier to be a coward. It took less courage to stay in hell than to try and find a way out of it.

I wanted to reach over to Rico, to draw him into my arms, stroke his hair and somehow soften the blow I'd just dealt him. I wanted to tell him he would be fine, that he'd find someone else far more deserving than me of the decent man he was. But I was afraid to touch him. I felt any physical contact of any kind now might be seen as my not meaning what I'd just said.

"Rico...Rico...are you going to be okay?" I asked him hesitantly. He looked up at me with tear-filled eyes.

"Is ... is there someone else?"

Oh, there was someone else all right but not the way he was thinking.

"No, Rico...there's no-one else. It's not that."

"Then what? There must be a reason. I just don't understand!"

His hurt was turning to a desperate anger, but I had no explanation.

"I...I'm sorry. I just can't explain. But this isn't because I'm interested in someone else, believe me!"

Rico blew his nose and regained some of his composure. He stared out the window, put the ring box in his pocket, and said:

"I almost wish you had said there was someone else. That would have been easier to understand than no reason at all."

We looked at each other and tears were close to the surface for us both. In my mind I saw another door closing, as he opened the car door and stepped back into the bright sunlight.

"See you around, " he said as he walked out of my life. "Thanks for the memories."

I started the car, tears pouring down my face. As I merged onto the highway, I wanted to floor the car and smash it into the guard rail or a bridge embankment. Yet even as I thought that, it stuck me what a mockery I was. I laughed sarcastically at the irony, the absurdity of the idea: me commit suicide? I was too gutless for that! I cried all the way home, washed my face hurriedly with cold water to try to remove the puffiness around my eyes.

Rico's shocked and pained face was still haunting me as my father walked through the door and I pasted on the false but expected smile of delight that hid my own self-disgust.

"Hi, daddy. How was your day?" I asked with the cheeriness he expected me to show on his arrival. The master was home. As I closed the door behind my father, I saw myself once again throwing away the keys to my prison. Would I ever be free of my master and leave this place called "home"?

CHAPTER 30: ADULT AT 21?

One of the things most often asked of women in an abusive situation is how and why did you put up with it for so long? If you hated it so much, if your life was so bad, why didn't you just get the hell out of there?

The answer to that is there isn't any one reason. There are hundreds of reasons, the biggest being fear: fear of the abuser, fear of being alone, fear of not having necessary survival skills, fear of non-acceptance by others, fear for others who might be hurt by the revelation (e.g. my mother) and fear that the hell you know may not be as bad as the hell you'll find out there. You become resigned, accepting that this is your lot in life. You know that if you play by his rules and don't make waves, you get by...that he'll even be nice to you. You convince yourself that it's not really so bad after all: there's a roof over your head, food to eat, T.V. for entertainment, and daydreams to escape into when the going gets rough. He's convinced you the world out there is a horrible place and you are so lucky to have him to protect you. So you get along by going along. Peace at any price.

But every once in a while, the compliant victim you've become rebels: you have been condemned to a life in prison for a crime you didn't commit. You were born free but you haven't been free to be yourself, to follow your heart, to act on your dreams for as long as you can remember. Somewhere deep inside, anger is a festering wound. Rage is building. You want to lash out at the abuser but your fear of him makes you lash out at yourself instead. You blame yourself, criticize yourself, hate yourself. Some victims resort to cutting, inflicting more pain on themselves, punishing themselves for someone else's sins. Others simply end it all by suicide. The rest, like me, keep hoping, believing that one day the abuser will come around, see what he has done, and that he truly does love you enough to finally set you free. That belief was what encouraged me to once again trust my father when he said:

"So, kitten, you're turning 21, becoming an adult. My little girl isn't a little girl any longer. So what do I give a 21-year-old for her birthday?"

His voice was kind, gentle, coaxing. My heart filled with hope. Could this be it? Was he finally going to set me free? I so wanted to believe that. I was about to blurt out "I want to be free to come and go as I please" but I hesitated. Years of my telling the truth had ended up in beatings or verbal whiplash. Would this be any different? He sensed my hesitation. He could smell my fear.

"Come on, kitten" he encouraged. "Tell daddy what you want. You're a grown woman now. It's time for you to speak up for yourself, to make your own decisions."

Somewhere in my head, alarm bells were going off. These words had a familiar ring. But I so wanted to believe that, at last, my time had come, that I had paid my dues, done my time, and he was truly about to set me free.

"Well, I...I really don't want anything in particular for my birthday...maybe some money to buy myself a new dress or something?" I faltered, too afraid to say what I'd really like.

"Oh, I don't mean that kind of thing, sweetheart!" He spoke so lovingly, so gently, that I began to relax. "Tell me what you REALLY want! I'm not blind or stupid. I know I've been hard on you. But I also know that at 21, you have the right to walk away from me and I have no right to hold you back. You are an adult, a grown woman. You are free to do what you want. So what do you want? Tell me... everything. Don't be afraid. I won't get mad!"

I bit the bullet. Rather, I took the bait. After ten horrible years, at last my "Daddy" was back. The desperate child in me welcomed him, even loved him, and most of all wanted to trust him. I did.

"Well," I started slowly, "since you say I'm an adult now and am free to do what I want, I'd like to come and go as I please..."

"And where would you be going?" He urged me on nicely.

"Oh, here and there...maybe out with some of my Uni friends once in a while...to a movie or a party...or just shopping with the girls. You know the kind of things girls do?"

"Yes, of course," he conceded. "Anything else?"

I spoke a little more warily on my next request, not yet fully trusting his relaxed, receptive face.

"Well...though it hasn't happened yet, if a guy were to ask me out, I'd like to think I could say yes without having to ask you?"

My heart skipped a few beats getting that one out, but he didn't bat an eye and I saw no twitch of his mouth to indicate he was getting angry.

"So is there someone you think might be interested enough in you to ask?" he pried.

"Oh, no!" I rushed my reply, just in case.

"Okay," he said. "That's fair enough. Is there anything else you want?"

I couldn't quite believe we were actually talking like this. Mom was nearby, trying to watch the TV. One minute she'd look at me nervously, her eyes seeming to warn me of imminent danger. Next minute, as he spoke quietly, gently, almost solicitously, she seemed to be encouraging me to speak up: this was my chance to finally be heard. Tell him! I relaxed even more. It felt so good to be talking openly like this.

"Well, there is one more thing I'd really like. One of my Uni friends, Gina, is getting married this summer and she's invited me to the wedding. I'd really like to go. I've never been to a wedding and..."

I never saw his hand move. I only felt it as it crashed into my face! My cheek was on fire and for a second I couldn't see. I brought up my arms to hide my face from the next blow I knew was coming, but I was too slow. His fist rammed into my ear and pain speared through my head. Somewhere I could hear mom crying, "Bogdan! Stop! What's the matter with you?! Stop!"

"What's the matter with ME?" he raged. "Filthy cunt! I give her everything and this is what she gives me back?" His voice dripped with anger and sarcasm.

"She wants! She wants!" he taunted. "She wants to do what she wants when she wants? She wants to date? She wants to go to a wedding? It's all about what she wants, filthy whore! What about what I want?"

Mom bravely tried again. "Well you did ask her! After all, she's 21! You told her to tell you what she wants."

He cut her off in mid-sentence. "What! Are you sticking up for her against me? Are you betraying me again? Sure! What could I expect from you...one filthy cunt gave birth to another one! She's just like you! Whores... both of you. Just whores!"

I was terrified. Tears poured down my face. I shook and shook, not so much from pain as from shock and disappointment. I had so wanted to trust him. I had so believed that at last my life was about to change. I wanted to vomit. I wanted to strike back at him. If I'd had a knife I might have plunged it in his eye. Or more likely, into myself. I couldn't go on like this!

Mom got up to leave. From some last vestige of courage, she said calmly to him as she walked out of the room:

"You are horrible, Bogdan! You are a horrible man! You call yourself a father? I don't know what you are but you are not a father!"

"And she is not my daughter!" he yelled after her. "A good daughter would show respect! Gratitude!" He had to have the last word.

"Go on!" he urged her. "Get out of here before I punch you too. You have nothing to say, whore! Once a whore, always a whore. I don't listen to whores. You have nothing to say in this! This is between her and me only! Get out!"

He was almost shrieking in his rage. His Mr. Hyde face was contorted in anger. His mouth twitched uncontrollably. I cowered beneath the blanket on that loathed bed chesterfield, bracing myself for more blows. They didn't come.

"Sit up!" he demanded. I obeyed, trying not to sniffle. I didn't dare look at him.

"Look at me, " he yelled, "when I'm talking to you! I'm not done with you yet! So, tell me again what it is you want!"

This time, I knew better: give him only the answers he wanted to hear. "Noth...nothing daddy. I don't want anything but you. I want only want you want for me. I'll do whatever you tell me to," I lied.

He didn't speak as he made himself calm down. I doubt he believed me but it made no difference. He had won again and he knew it. Neither of us spoke for a few minutes. I waited. What was next?

"You know what I say to all your wants don't you?" he asked.

"Yes, daddy?" I replied meekly, still hoping somewhat that he might surprise me. Stupid idea!

"NO!" he shouted. "The answer is NO to all your requests. What do you think? That just because you're 21, you can do what you want? As long as you live in my house, under my roof, and I provide for you, you do what I want and what I tell you to! Will you be a good daughter or do I have to keep punishing you and beating you like I had to do with your mother till I finally kicked the devil out of her? Is that what you want me to do?"

"No daddy...I'll be a good daughter...I promise..."

Then, just as suddenly as he'd lashed out thirty minutes earlier, he turned soft and kind all over again. He looked at me gently and opened his arms, beckoning me to come into them. Inside, I was cringing: I wanted arms around me but not his. I knew what followed his rages. But I also knew resistance was futile. I moved into his arms.

His voice was soothing as he said:

"Come, come my little one. Come to daddy. Daddy gave you a hard time tonight but I was just testing you... testing your love."

He pulled me closer. He was aroused, pressing himself against me. "Let's give mom a bit more time to fall asleep."

He lifted the blanket and forced my head down toward his crotch. He undid his fly and his erect penis sprung out. Covering it and my head lightly with the blanket, he cooed:

"You know what daddy wants you to do, don't you darling. Make daddy a happy man now."

SHELL

She hides behind the shell
She has built around herself
A beautiful doll now broken
And long ago left on a shelf

If you shake her up she rattles
Shards of innocence loose inside
A painted smile on porcelain lips
Where lonely tears have dried

Her responses sometimes harsh
Have been shaped by years of violence
Her porcelain shell of protection
So fragile beneath her silence

If she snaps at you, forgive her
Behind the anger lie her tears
She cries when no-one's near her
It's been that way for years

Be patient with her! She's trying.
She will come down from that shelf
Once she finds that voice that frees her
And begins to love herself

©*Viga Boland, 2012*

CHAPTER 31: THE WORKING WORLD

My university graduation, just like my Grade 8 graduation was a non-event. I attended none of the formal activities nor the after-parties. The friends I'd made at University moved out of my life and on with their own lives. Some got married. Some travelled overseas. I did what my father had planned for me to do. I landed a teaching position in a Catholic girls' high school and my father decided with the added income I'd now be bringing in, it was time we moved out of the duplex and into a nicer home in a suburb close to the school.

We purchased a beautiful ranch bungalow in a better class, but older neighborhood of Etobicoke. Mom and I loved the house and my father's face swelled with pride as friends came to visit. Our new home, was without doubt, the nicest of the friends' homes and when visitors left, my father would gloat for hours about how we showed them all up. When they had asked how we could afford a home like this on their factory wages, he'd proudly tell them I was helping them pay the mortgage.

"What do you mean?" asked Frank, such a dear friend, the kind of father I wished I had. "Is Viga paying you rent now? Isn't it time she was on her own with her own place?"

"And why would she do something like that?" my father retorted smugly. "She's a smart girl. She knows that this way she can live cheaply, and in the end, whatever she has contributed to the mortgage will come back to her."

"So how much is she contributing?" Frank persisted.

"Her whole paycheque, of course," my father announced proudly. Frank looked shocked so my father hastily added:

"She knows it will all be hers when we die and besides, living at home she has minimal expenses! Like I said, smart girl!" He tapped his temple to reinforce the notion I had a brain and used it. I couldn't help but think if I had half a brain, I wouldn't still be living at home and putting up with my father!

Frank looked at me. His face was incredulous but he read the warning in my face. There was no point pursuing this. My Father had made his decisions about my future, my paycheques and my life. As long as I was under my parents' roof, every penny I earned went into the family bank account to which only he had access. As our pays came in, mom and I handed over the cheques to my Father. But in recognition of my new status as a working woman who brought home a weekly wage, he generously raised our allowances to five dollars a week. I nearly choked as mom and I smothered him with kisses and "thank you papas" for his overwhelming kindness and he patted our heads like two puppies saying, "That's alright, my girls! See, when you're good to papa, papa is good to you." UGH!

And so my life trudged on. I had given up any hope anything would ever change and accepted my lot in life as my father's secret mistress. I was resigned to the fact that, after my failed attempt at freedom at 21, I would become an old maid servicing my father's sexual needs. Every so often, just to make sure I never told my mother, he'd remind me how hurt she would be to find out how I'd deceived her all those years. Or he'd play his other card, saying she'd never believe me anyway since I'd never told her in all that time, and after all, if I wasn't happy with my life, she'd wonder why I hadn't left long ago. As he snidely confided:

"She's not a bright woman but she's not that stupid either!"

Somehow I never found a strong enough argument to his statements. Argument seemed so futile and never led to more than another bout of his anger and verbal abuse reminding me what an ungrateful daughter I was, that I was so ugly no man would want me anyway! Wasn't I lucky he wanted me? And thus, the brainwashed woman-child he'd cultivated so cleverly over the years backed away from any thoughts of freedom time and again.

My only joy over those next couple of years came from teaching. I lived for the classroom and my students. The minute I stepped into the building, waved good morning to students and greeted the staff, I became someone else. This person was reasonably confident, friendly and outgoing and loved by her students. They were my world. I lived for their moments of sudden understanding, their ideas brought on by classroom discussion, their laughter and their trust in me as their teacher and friend. They filled a deep hole inside my heart and soul, made me feel loved for who I was. They were the only thing that made me feel good about myself, worthy and worthwhile. Finally life had some meaning.

I taught English, Latin and Math to Grade 9 and 10, and one of the best parts about it all was that it meant my evenings were too busy with reading compositions and preparing classes to sit night after night on that despised chesterfield watching T.V. It also meant my Father had to settle for less sex on demand, sometimes only getting it once a week. That suited me fine. None at all would have been even better but that was too much to hope for. Now and then, he'd complain and I'd brightly suggest he try mom for a change...or for good.

"Now how would that look?" he'd ask me. "She's stupid but not that stupid!" he'd repeat. "She would wonder why suddenly I want sex with her after I haven't touched her in months."

"Oh, so you do still have sex with her then?" I asked curiously.

"Well of course I do once in a while just to keep her from becoming suspicious. But it would look strange if suddenly I wanted her more frequently, wouldn't it?"

Then, to my disgust, he'd add "Besides, she doesn't turn me on. I have to force myself to make love to her."

That would make my stomach turn. I wanted to hit him, lash out at him. She was my mother, my poor little mom who worked day in and day out, long hours at Christies Biscuits, handing over her weekly pay-cheque to him, cooking his meals, doing his washing, and catering to his needs, ever fearful of his temper and sudden tantrums, just as I was. She was nothing to him but a slave and he didn't even desire her as a woman. How had I so replaced her in his heart? She deserved so much more from life.

At the same time, I'd be silently angry at them both. How could she not see what was going on? Was she really as stupid as he said? How could she not wonder why a man with his sexual appetite went for months without wanting sex with her? She knew he wasn't having affairs. He was always home. She also knew how insanely possessive he was of me, how controlling. Did she never wonder why he wouldn't let me date? Could she really be that stupid?

Now in hindsight, I have to ask myself if mom really didn't know. All these years I have excused her not helping me, believing she really didn't know, that we'd hidden the secret that well. But now I am not so sure. In the last year of her life, when we finally became close for the first time, I asked her if she knew. She insisted she truly had no idea. She said friends had hinted at it but she had told them and herself no way could this be going on. Now, at 67 years of age, older and wiser myself, for the first time I think mama knew. But like all the others whose stories I've read where the mothers didn't step in to help their abused daughters, she lived in denial: the reality would have been more than she could handle. She too didn't want to believe the man she'd married, the natural father of her child, could do this to his own daughter. And being uneducated, unworldly, and so reliant on my Father for everything, coupled with her lack of independence, self-esteem and confidence, she wouldn't have known what to do to get me out of that situation anyway. So she closed her eyes and mind to it all, especially since I never once brought it up with her. That is how much my father had convinced me there was nothing to be achieved by telling mom any of it.

CHAPTER 32: MY AUSSIE "KNIGHT"

I was in my second year of teaching when my world turned completely upside down. Little did I know when the principal of the school excitedly announced in our first staff meeting after the Christmas break, that our previously all-female staff was now to include two male members, that the door to my freedom had suddenly swung wide open, but it would be up to me to have the courage to walk through it. Two gentlemen stood up as she welcomed them to St. Joseph's: one, a short, dark, rather unkempt looking European with a complicated name; the second, a tall, suntanned, sandy-haired blonde whose handsome face looked slightly confused and quite uncomfortable as thirty pairs of women's eyes appraised him. And in the split-second it took for me to look at him, I heard that ominous voice inside my head warn: "Girl! You're in trouble!"

The next two days, each time I ducked into the staffroom to grab a book or use the washroom, my eyes darted quickly around the room to see if the blond was there. At lunchtime the second day, I was rewarded with my first sighting since the staff-meeting. He was huddled in a corner talking with Mike, the other new addition. One of the other, very friendly married female teachers breezed into the staffroom, and addressed them both:

"Hey! There's our new additions! Welcome gentlemen! Where are you both from?"

Mike was the first to speak as the blonde again looked slightly stunned and unsure of himself. When he finally replied, again alarm bells sounded in my head.

"I'm John, and I'm from Australia, from Merewether Beach in Newcastle," he replied proudly in a strong Australian accent that charmed the ladies, myself included.

"Oh, where's Newcastle?" asked another teacher, and the conversation kept flowing around our two new male members. They wanted to know all about them. Were they married, kids, etc. The ladies were all a-twitter like a bunch of birds excited to have found some crumbs on the ground. I don't think I heard much of it after John's initial reply. All I could hear was that warning voice in my head telling me to steer clear of him. He was too good-looking and from what I could gather, single. I averted my eyes, leaned over a narrow counter, opened a book, and bit into my sandwich, standing awkwardly near the staffroom door, ready to bolt if he came anywhere near me. I was reaching for my coat to go to the next class, when I sensed a presence beside me and was taken aback as a male voice asked:

"Can I help you with that?"

I turned to look into a pair of grey-green eyes that seemed to twinkle with amusement, and told the warning voice inside me to shut up as I blurted out with a confidence I didn't feel:

"G'day mate!"

Now it was John's turn to be taken aback. He looked at me in surprise and asked, "You're not...an Aussie are you?"

"Sure am!" I replied brightly, like the most self-assured woman in the world. Such an actress! Hand her an Oscar! "I grew up in Sydney. Yagoona/Bankstown area. But I've lived in Canada since I was 11."

John looked thrilled to meet another Aussie. As I would learn, he was a true-blue, proud Aussie who loved his homeland with a fervor second to none and would always want to go home. But as our paths crossed and joined in that staffroom, it would be years, not months as he'd originally planned, before he got to go home again. I had just met, and in one look and one short exchange, fallen head over heels in love with my husband-to-be and he with me.

As he helped me into my coat and I sensed his nearness, my pulse raced and my face burned with excitement. I almost floated down the hall to my next class with my mind on anything but the upcoming lesson. All I could hear was that ominous voice in my head telling me I was in trouble, but part of me welcomed the trouble. I needed it if I was ever to have a normal life. I told the voice to get lost and instead, kept conjuring up those grey-green eyes, that handsome, suntanned face and the rush I'd felt as he'd helped me into my coat. John was no Rico and I knew there was no running away from this.

John's entrance into the confused, unhappy, sordid and secret world in which I'd lived for the past ten or more years threw me into chaos. Initially, we'd only chat over lunch in that tiny, crowded staffroom. As we drew each other into each other's lives, it was as if the room were empty. The world was just the two of us. I was overwhelmed by his presence, his nearness, his masculinity. His face would suddenly pop into my head during quiet times in the classroom while the students worked on their math. I'd daydream like a teenager with her first big crush. I was happier than ever heading off to work in the morning, but filled more and more with dread and loathing every time I stepped back inside the house after school. All I could think of was where, when and how would all this end up. And as if he sensed something, my father became more and more probing about how things were at school.

"So how is that kangaroo fitting in at the school?" My father sarcastically asked.

I'd told my parents about the two new male additions to the staff. My father had immediately dismissed Mike, the European, since he was married, but almost daily he'd question me about John, and always snidely and with derision. I'd brush off his curiosity with a quick "Fine...I guess...I don't see him much," and I'd consider myself lucky that at least he couldn't very well show up at the school to check on me as he'd done a few years earlier on campus.

"Just another gold-digger coming to Canada hoping to find some rich girlfriend to live off!" my father would remark, and I'd cringe at his ability to so readily judge someone he'd never met, someone who made my head spin. Oh, what had I gotten myself into? If my father were to find out just how much I already knew about John and the effect he was having on me, his snide remarks would soon turn to rage. My happiness at seeing John each morning was being dampened each evening by my growing sense of panic and fear of what would come of it all.

And of course, the fear was increasing with each question John was asking me too. While he was telling me lots about himself and his family, I was saying very little about mine. How could I tell him? What would I tell him? Inevitably, he did what I'd been dreading: he asked me for a date.

"So! What about a movie on Friday night?"

"Er...um...Friday night...no I have to take mom to get groceries," I fibbed. Mom didn't drive so now that I did, my father left the driving to me, especially when they went to their adult, whisky-breath parties.

"Well then, how about I take you out to dinner on Saturday night? Do you like Chinese food?"

"I...I don't know..." I said. My mind was frantically trying to come up with another excuse for why I couldn't go out with him. "I've never eaten Chinese. Our background is European. Chinese food just isn't our thing. Is Chinese food popular in Australia?" I babbled on, trying to steer the conversation away from a date.

"Yes it is, but okay then, you pick. You must know some good places to eat around here. I'm sure other fellas have taken you to some nice restaurants?"

I wanted to laugh, but it wasn't funny. Here I was, 22 years old and I'd never been on a date. I didn't count that sad, arranged Graduation dance as a true date. I wouldn't even know how to act on a date! Would we hold hands in a movie? Kiss? Should I let him kiss me? What was appropriate? I was more naive about such things than the teenagers I was teaching!

And so it went for months, John trying to get me out on a date, me avoiding the subject and giving unsatisfactory reasons for not going out with him. I began to fear I'd lose him. When I saw him joking and chatting with one or two of the other single female staffers, I was overwhelmed by jealousy, hurt and confusion.

Couldn't they see he was mine? No, of course not.

And what was I to him? I thought he was keen on me too. So why was he flirting with them?

He was flirting because he wasn't mine. He couldn't even get me to go on a date with him! My father's voice would taunt me: he was just an Aussie kangaroo, trying to date me so he could get into my pants. My father was right. I was so naive, so brainwashed, so insecure. Of course! Why would this handsome, suntanned man be interested in me? I was ugly, dirty, soiled goods. Something only my Father could want.

I started telling myself it was time to break this off, find some story John would believe, tell him I wasn't interested in dating him, something, anything but the truth. I felt so desperate. I was in love and I was trapped. But as I'd proved to myself so many times before, I was also a coward: it would be easier to walk away from John than to tell my father about him. Gutless, despicable coward.

"I am what I think I am"

CHAPTER 33: DUMB BLONDE

As the school year drew to a close, I dreaded the long summer break ahead. John had landed a job coaching sports at a summer youth camp outside Toronto and would be gone all summer. Part of me was relieved, a very small part. Most of me wanted to die at the thought of not seeing him day after day. He wouldn't even be able to call me. My father would know. He couldn't write to me as my father opened my mail. I had no privacy. I never had had any.

Even though I was a grown woman, my father would walk in on me while I was changing, or while I was in the shower. If my bedroom door was closed, he never knocked. I was questioned about every phone call and if a half-hour shopping took an hour, my reason for the delay was questioned. If we were all at the local deli together and my father caught the good-looking server winking at me, I was grilled mercilessly at home, accused of flirting with him, reminded of the whore I was and how disgusting my behaviour had been. Now that I was older, my father had tightened my shackles even more and watched my every move. Though he never said it, he obviously feared the inevitable: one day I just might grow up and run away and he used the only way he knew to prevent that: he kept fueling my fear of him.

It was mom who helped me stay in touch with John over that summer break. While I had told my father nothing about John, dear little mama knew everything. For the first time in my life, she had become an ally, a somewhat unwilling one, but only from the angle that she was as terrified as I was as to where this was all headed and half- wished it would all go away. As I talked to her more and more about John, showed her a wallet-sized photo I had of him (and hid it deeply beneath some clothes in my drawer) she looked at me sadly and nervously:

"My girl...you are in love!"

I'd try to deny it. "No, mom...I...I just enjoy talking with him. He tells me all about the Australia I've never seen and..."

"Oh, stop it Viga," Mom smiled sadly. "Stop it! You

ARE in love!" she insisted and I knew she was right. "So what are you going to do about it?"

"What do you think I should do?" I asked, knowing there was only one answer but lacking the courage to do it.

"You have to tell your father. You know that! It's time anyway. How long are you going to keep living with us? You need your own life. The girls at work can't believe you still live at home now that you are teaching. They can't believe you never go out, don't have a boyfriend. They even ask me if there's something wrong with you!"

Oh great! So there it was now. Even other people, people I didn't know thought I was weird. Didn't anyone, including mom, ever think there just might be another reason, another person behind my loner status?

"Oh mom, you know how dad is! He'll freak! I don't know how to tell him. I'm scared! Could...could you tell him?"

Mom turned away. "He'll be home in a few minutes and I have to have dinner ready. We better talk about this some other time. This just puts us both in a bad mood and he will pick up on it as soon as he walks through the door. Time to put our smiles on." And she turned back to frying the pork chops.

Five minutes later, we heard the garage door go up and we positioned ourselves in our usual spots: she, aproned, smiling, in front of the stove ready for his quick, dismissive peck on the cheek; me, positioned by the back door, like the slave ready to greet her master, smile in place, trying to get my mind off John and swallowing my fear as my father's eyes intently probed my face, looking for I don't know what as I greeted him at the door:

"You look different. Aren't you happy to see me? Did something happen today? What's up?"

"Noth...nothing happened today, daddy. Just another day." I lied. He was the last person I'd tell about the quick kiss John and I stole out of sight of the students as we said goodbye. No way could I tell him how I trembled at the touch of that "kangaroo" or how my heart sank at the thought he'd be gone all summer. "I'm just tired. Teaching is quite exhausting, you know. Here are your slippers. I have them ready for you."

John and I stayed in touch that summer with the help of mom and one of her supervisors at work. He wrote me letters and mailed them to the supervisor's address. She gave the letters to my mom for me. I'd rush to read them, then I'd share them with mom. And before my Father got home, I'd bury them deeply in different drawers, taking them out to re-read whenever he wasn't home. I clung desperately to those little pieces of John, pulling out his photo, kissing it and dreaming that one day we just might be together forever.

Over that summer John grew a short beard that I didn't like and I went blond which John did like. He had often told me how his ideal woman was a tall, slender blonde with long legs and a flat tummy. I was none of those things. If anything I was so much the opposite. I was only 5' 2", with a curvy body, short legs and a typical European belly that I loathed! John being attracted to me made no sense at all in my opinion. And given my deep insecurity, my now ingrained belief that I was ugly, dirty and unlovable, it was hard for me to conceive he'd stick around for long, especially since we never dated or did anything that normal couples do. In fact, I don't even remember now what lame excuses I gave him for not being able to date, and even after we'd been married for years I still had dreams that he'd found someone else. Yet, he came back after that summer camp looking as happy to see me as I was to see him, beard and all.

"What's that on your face!" I blurted in shock when I saw him.

"I got lazy over summer, " he laughingly replied. "Like it?"

"Well...no, not really. Are you going to keep it?"

"We'll see how it goes," John said. "Love the hair! How'd that happen? Going to keep it?" he teased.

I didn't explain the hair. I had just been desperate to be his ideal woman and that was the only part I could do anything about. What I also didn't share with him was how my father had handled my desire to go blond all of a sudden.

"Why do you want to be a blond?" he'd asked suspiciously when he spotted the bottle of dye in the bathroom.

"Ah...just want a change," I lied. "Mom dyes her hair. Lots of women do. Just for fun I guess to see how I'd look as a blond..."

"Well, I like you just the way you are! I don't like phony women with phony hair, makeup and all that stuff! I like my woman natural!"

I wanted to scream at him: "But I am not YOUR woman! You don't own me!" But of course I didn't have the guts to do it. I looked at him weakly, afraid to go ahead, silently asking permission at 22 years of age to dye my hair!

"Oh, go on" he said suddenly. "It will be interesting to see what you look like I guess. I'll even help you do it."

I nearly choked, but I let him help me apply the dye, wiping it as it ran down my face, and even blowing it dry for me. I felt so smothered by his attention I was cringing inside but I didn't dare rebuff his offer of help. When it was done, I wasn't sure I liked the new me: without makeup, I looked somewhat washed out. But my father liked it too much. Out of earshot of my mom, he whispered:

"Ooh...you look so sexy! If only your mother wasn't here right now. Your new look makes me horny!"

His words brought bile into my throat. I was sickened by his response, his filthy whisper. His desire for me simply repulsed me and as I'd noticed more and more since falling in love with John, my father's presence was disgusting me more than it ever had. I was becoming increasingly disgusted with myself too. When I was with John, I felt almost giddy, innocent. But then I had to come home night after night and mutate back into being my father's whore. I'd fall into a troubled sleep wondering how much longer I could go on deceiving not one, but both men now, as I bounced from the man I loved back to the man who was my unwanted lover. Deceiving John was even harder for me to live with than deceiving my father. It made me feel dirtier than ever.

"Let's take some photos of you with the new hair," suggested my father brightly. "What do you think mama? Do you like your daughter's new look?"

Mom just looked at him with her usual look of disgust which he rarely noticed as he was always so much more focused on me. She said nothing. She never did. What difference would what she thought make? He never asked or wanted her opinion on anything important and this was far from important.

"I'm going to bed," she announced without looking at either of us.

As soon as she had left the room, my father suggested I find something better to wear for the photos. I put on a business dress. He snapped a few shots.

"Got anything more interesting to wear?" he asked.

"Like what?" What would I have on that $5 a week allowance he so generously gave us? I used it to buy material to sew my own clothes with when I'd saved up enough!

"Oh, you must have something," he prompted. "Maybe a nice tight fitting sweater?" He winked suggestively.

I came back with another of mom's snug-fitting sweater dresses.

"Oh, yeah..." he crooned, turning himself on as he snapped the pictures. I was bristling with anger. I'd dyed my hair for John and now it was making my father horny. That dirty feeling was crawling all over me again. He came close to me and pulled me to him, forcing me to feel his erection.

"Go find a sexy nightie," he whispered huskily. "Hope your mother's asleep by now. I can't hold off much longer!"

As I walked toward my bedroom to find something "sexy" I wondered how had this gone so wrong! I wanted to cry. I wanted to scream. I wanted to run. I wanted John to be saying these things to me, not my own father! Had I known dying my hair would have brought this result, I would never had done it. I decided that soon as I could, I'd dye it back to its mousy brown, but not before John had seen it. There had to be some good in all the bad. As it was, I remained blonde till long after our wedding day because the man I loved liked it. And for him, I'd do anything, including, finally, asking my father to set me free.

CHAPTER 34: PROPOSAL PRESSURES

John proposing to me has long been one of his favorite stories and it happened even before the blond hair. He had only been at the school one month. We were sitting beside each other in that cramped lunchroom when he suddenly looked at me in a dreamy way and blurted out, but only loudly enough for me to hear:

"Will you marry me?"

I was stunned, so stunned I blurted back an unthinking, "Yes!"

It wasn't exactly a romantic setting but for those few moments no-one else in that room, or even the world, existed. It was like those first few seconds when you wake up: everything's temporarily blurry and then you slowly begin to focus. When my vision finally cleared, I began to panic deep inside. What had I just done? I'd told a man I'd marry him and I had no idea how on earth I could do that! How could I now tell him marriage was out of the question, that it was never going to happen for me, not with him, not with anyone, ever! I was already married...to my father!

John was smiling, chatting on happily about how, when and where we would be married, squeezing my hand under the table out of sight of the other teachers, and I was barely hearing a word he was saying. My mind was racing faster than my heart: I barely knew him! We'd never even been alone together! What did I really know about him? Maybe he was a nutcase! After all, who proposes to a woman he's only known one month, a woman he's never dated? Was he out of his mind? I most certainly must be for saying "yes" given my situation! Everything after that is a bit of a blur. I don't remember how we ended the conversation but I do know when I left for the next class I was in turmoil. Instead of feeling happy, I was filled with dread.

I spent the next few days worrying how I was going to get myself out of this mess. I wished the day I'd first said "G'day mate!" to that handsome tanned Aussie had never happened. Why did he have to come into my life? I was almost angry, but mostly at myself for letting this happen. Why had I let it go this far? I was really just an immature kid in a woman's body, enjoying the romance of it all. I told myself I wasn't in love. I was just infatuated, buoyed on by having a good-looking male flirt with me.

I told myself that he too was kidding himself. He was most likely, as my father was always saying, just another hot guy looking for a good lay. After all, he was new to Canada, alone, running away from some girl at home in Australia who had wanted to marry him. He couldn't possibly really want to marry this ugly woman who let her father have his way with her. And ultimately, if he truly were serious about marrying me, if he was typical of all Aussies, sooner or later he'd want to go home. They always did. He was already saying that once we were married we'd move back to Australia and raise our children on the beach. But I didn't want to leave the world I knew for one I didn't. As bad as it was, I was used to it now. And even though we weren't all that close, I really couldn't bear the thought of leaving my mother. I went through all the usual kind of thinking that holds back a person so frightened to face an unknown future i.e. easier to stay with the devil you know that go with the one you don't!

As the weeks, months wore on, despite all my misgivings, despite all my negative self-talk, despite desperately searching for a way to back out of that too-hasty "Yes" I'd given him, one thing became evident: John was serious about marrying me. The time for decisions, actions and the ultimate horror was approaching: I would have to tell my father about John. I was utterly and completely terrified.

Telling my father didn't happen quickly. That would take a year of making lame excuses to John for why we couldn't date, snatched moments of passion in the school janitor's closet during school vacation, or even getting poor mom to accompany us to a movie when my father was on night shift. That was the only way I could get out of the house on an evening as my father phoned home every night at 8pm for a 30-minute chat, five minutes with mom and twenty-five minutes with me! I knew why he phoned home every night: he was checking up on me.

Ever since I'd told him about John's addition to our staff, my father had found a way to ask about him. Was he still at the school? Had he gone back to Australia yet? Was he planning to? When? How come I didn't know much about him? Surely we must talk? Did he appeal to me? Would I like to go out with him? On and on, week after week. His habit of searching my face, my eyes, looking for lies or unhappiness when he arrived home from work, the same questions day after day had intensified.

"What's wrong?" he'd start almost as soon as he'd walk through the door. "Did something happen at school today?"

"No. Why?"

"You look strange." Or "You look unhappy."

"I'm fine! Nothing happened!"

"Well, you don't look happy to see me!" The guilt-trip probe.

"Of course I'm happy to see you," I'd lie, wishing the grilling would stop. How could any sane person think a 23-year old woman would be happy with the constant suspicion, needling, doubting? How could any reasonable, normal father think a 23-year-old would be happy living in a jail, servicing her father's sexual needs, never being allowed to go out, to spend time with people her own age, or to even have friends with whom to spend time! But then, he wasn't reasonable nor normal.

And most of the time, as I'd often found over the years, I doubted my own normalcy too. I was weird, an oddball. Sadly, I was an oddball in love with a normal, nice guy and increasingly torn between trying to find the courage to tell my father the truth or tell John to get out of my life and go find himself a nice, normal woman.

Then there was mom to think about:

"Viga, how much longer is this going to go on? I'm becoming a nervous wreck!"

My poor mom looked at me in despair. We had just watched John drive away after spending a few hours with me cuddling in our basement while my Father was on night shift. Mom had been "on watch". She would stand nervously by the kitchen window from the time John arrived, watching for my father's car.

Over the past year my father's migraines, which had begun around the time he started molesting me 12 years prior, had intensified. He was now getting them two to three times a month. They were so severe he couldn't work. That meant any time of day or night he could suddenly arrive home. The possibility of him doing so terrified both mom and me, especially when John stopped in to visit. We'd come so close to being caught on one occasion that I nearly vomited in fear as I watched John's car pull away down the street as my father pulled into our driveway. Both mom and I were nervous wrecks that night. Fortunately, my father was in such pain with his migraine he didn't notice our panic- stricken faces when he bolted through the door and headed for the bathroom to throw up. I actually felt sorry for my father when he had the migraines: he suffered fiercely, often for 36-72 hours. It always amazed and confused me that I still cared when he was in pain. Yet, at the same time I felt slightly evil as I inwardly rejoiced at the fact he'd leave me alone in every way during those times.

Mom wasn't the only one putting pressure on me to tell my father about John. As another school year drew to a close, John asked the same question:

"How much longer are we going to go on like this, never dating, stealing moments together on a basement mattress while your mom keeps watch, even taking your mom with us wherever we go somewhere as some kind of cover ... and for what? What is going on here? What is the problem with your dad? Why can't you tell him about us? What are you SO afraid of?"

I looked at John with despair. I so wanted to tell him the truth but I was more terrified of what his reaction might be than of telling my father. For sure, I would lose him. He would be disgusted, revolted to know not only was my father having sex with me but that it had been going on for 12 years and was still going on now while he and I we were talking marriage!

I told myself John couldn't possibly want such soiled goods. I was raised in the era where virginity was the greatest gift you could give your husband but my father had made sure that was one gift I could never give. John had been raised in a good Catholic home. Half his family were priests, brothers or nuns. He still attended Mass every Sunday. He'd never understand why I had let this happen or continue for so many years. I couldn't give him the real answer to his question.

"I...I don't know." I stammered miserably. "I can't explain. I really can't. There are problems in my home, big problems that I can't tell you or anyone about. Please try to understand...please!" I pleaded.

"I've been trying to understand for months now," John said gently. "And I've been patient, haven't I? But Viga, I love you and I want to marry you. I want us to spend the rest of our lives together. I want us to have children ... all the usual things. I'm nearing 30. I've found the woman I want to share my life with..."

He broke off and inside I was breaking. I wanted all those things too and I wanted them with John. Sooner or later I would have to make that decision I'd been avoiding: tell my father and face the consequences, even if it meant he might kill me. And I honestly believed he would. Or tell John to get out of my life forever. At that point, I wished the earth would just swallow me up: I was THAT scared of either choice.

CHAPTER 35: CHICKENING OUT

Toward the end of that year, one of the staff, a Polish woman whom my parents had met through me, decided to hold a year-end staff party. I wanted to attend. My father didn't like the idea at all. For some reason, because the staffer was Polish and because they had met, he felt they should be invited too. I had a devil of a time convincing him it was inappropriate for him to attend a staff party. Eventually he spat out his real concern:

"Will that f-ing kangaroo be there?" His face twitched angrily as he asked.

"How would I know? He might be. It's a staff party after all. The nuns and priests who teach at both schools are invited too!" St. Joes (for girls) and Michael Power (for boys) were adjacent schools and the staff taught in both.

"How come you don't know?" he asked sarcastically. "You work with him. Are you trying to tell me you never see him or talk to him?"

"We are in different departments, dad! He's in science. I'm in English! He mainly teaches at Michael Power! Our paths rarely cross!" I responded, hoping he wouldn't detect the lie. Of course John would be there! I'd mastered the art of lying to my Father over the years, but he remained ever suspicious of me, increasingly so since John had joined the staff. I wonder now if he somehow had sensed a change in me that I didn't think was obvious. Like I said way back, he was not a stupid man and even prided himself on being very good reader of people.

As his face twitched angrily searching for some valid reason to prevent me from attending a staff function, my own anger was rising. Here I was, 23 years old, asking permission to go to a party with my work associates! I felt years of pent-up rage rising to the top. Between the pressure I was getting from both mom and John and my own growing need to get away from all this, being held in check only by my tremendous fear of my father, I was reaching a breaking point. I might have spat it all out then and there, but suddenly he said:

"Well I suppose it might look bad for you if the nuns and priests attend and you don't. So okay... "

My Father's need for our family to look good in everyone else's eyes was, for sure, the only reason he was agreeing to let me go.

"But be home by midnight! Mama and I don't want to be kept up waiting for you." Any excuse!

"Dad!" I said. "You don't need to wait up, for heavens sake! Wanda only lives five kilometers from here! You've been to her house. Nothing's going to happen to me! And I'm not much of a drinker. So what are you worried about? Just go to bed!"

My Father's face began twitching again. "Just be home by midnight, okay? You've pushed me this far. Don't push me further or I might change my mind. Now go!"

I didn't wait to hear more. I was out the door in a flash and ten minutes later I was standing beside my beloved fiancée sharing drinks and laughter with the staff. By now, the whole school knew we were engaged. John and I had somehow managed to get away to Toronto one night when my father was working and together, we'd shopped for my ring, a simple, but lovely solitaire. I kept the ring hidden at home, slipping it lovingly on my finger once I got to the school. The first day I wore it in class, I was like a giddy teen. I couldn't wait to see if my students would spot it. Suddenly, one did. I saw her lean over to another student and whisper. I caught that student looking surprised and smiling, and by the time the bell ended that period, a little crowd of giggling girls had gathered around my desk.

"Miss...is...is that an engagement ring on your finger?" The anticipation of my response on their faces was matched only by my own joyous anticipation as I gushed, "Yes!"

The room erupted in delighted schoolgirl squeals and giggles.

"Oh wow! Told you so...!"

"See! I was right!"

"Can...can we look at your ring?"

And then, of course came the question they most wanted to ask.

"Who's the lucky guy? Is it someone on the staff."

By now I was grinning like a Cheshire Cat. "Uh-hum..."

"Who...who?"

"Who do you think?"

"It's Mr. B. isn't it," stated Sandy, one of the more assured students.

"You got it!" I exclaimed proudly, trying to contain my own giddy excitement, and trying simultaneously to quieten that inner warning voice again that was reminding me that this news would now get out and I would have hell to pay if my father learned of it through someone other than me.

Of course the news spread like wildfire through both schools and now, at the party, as John and I chatted with staff members about when our wedding would take place, again I kept pushing away that ominous voice that reminded me my father didn't yet know just how far along this entire thing had come and that I really couldn't keep it from him much longer.

As the clock neared midnight, I said to John that I had to go. He wouldn't let me. We were having such a good time, doing something normal couples in love do, sharing drinks and chatter with friends, in the open! No, he insisted. I couldn't leave yet. It was still so early for a party that had only started a couple of hours earlier!

Rebelling inside, fighting that warning voice, telling myself I had a right to stay and enjoy myself, I bolstered my courage with another glass of wine John insisted I have, and hung in there. Around 1 a.m. my nerves got the better of me.

"John, I HAVE to go!" I insisted. "Where's my coat?"

We dug through the pile of coats tossed onto Wanda's bed and as John helped me into it, he wrapped his big muscular arms around me and hugged me close.

"I wish I could just pick you up and take you home to my place," he whispered huskily as he began kissing me. Desire surged through me, desire like I'd never felt before. Oh, how I wished I could go home with him too and never see my father again. But I pushed John away.

"I've gotta go," I said weakly. "I've got to go! Now!"

The snow had pelted down over the past few hours and it took quite a long time to clean off my car and get it out from between the other cars that had parked me in. I drove home slowly, very on edge on the slippery roads. But the tension mounting inside me had little to do with the roads. I hadn't even shut off the engine when my Father bolted into the garage, his face red with rage. He flung open the door to my car and spat at me:

"Where the fuck have you been!" he screamed at me. He grabbed my coat and started pulling me out of the car. "Fucking whore!"

He pushed me roughly through the back door of the garage. Suddenly, I felt a stinging whack across the back of my neck. He had grabbed the long-handled snowbrush as he'd pushed me through the garage. Now he had slammed it into my neck so hard I was seeing stars and my head was reeling in pain.

"I told you to be home by midnight! It's 1:30! Where the fuck were you? Were you with that fucking kangaroo?" He punched me hard again in the back of the head as he shoved me inside the house.

"I...I...was stuck in the sn...snow!" I protested weakly. "We...we couldn't get my car out from between the other cars. I had to ask people to come out and move their cars."

"Stop lying, you cunt!" he raged at me. "Can't you tell time? Didn't you know it was snowing? If you knew you had to be home by midnight, you should have been leaving at 11:30! So, now, fucking cunt, where were you?"

"Bogdan! Bogdan! Stop swearing!" my mama implored from the kitchen. She was nervously shredding a Kleenex and had obviously been crying.

"What is so bad? She's a grown woman." She persevered bravely, defending me, knowing all too well how violent he could become when he was in one of these rages. He turned to her, angrily, his arm and fist rising as if to strike her now. Instead, he yelled:

"You ... yes, YOU would defend her against me, your husband, wouldn't you! One whore protecting another! Once a whore, always a whore, and she is just like you! That's what you gave birth to: another lying, cheating whore like yourself!"

His filthy words were ringing in my ears. My throbbing head was spinning with the expletives. But he was far from finished with either of us. The blow to my neck was burning and the pain in my head was fierce. I started to cry. My tears brought a kick to my backside that knocked me over. Again, my mom protested.

"Bogdan, stop! Are you crazy? What are you trying to do? Kill her?"

"Shut your filthy mouth, woman!" he spat back at her. "Get out of here before I let you have it too! This is none of your business! I told you long ago, this is between her and me! Now get out! Go to bed! You have nothing to say!"

Mom looked at me with such sadness. I knew she was trying to apologize for not being able to help me with him. She started out of the room and once more, tried bravely to end the scene.

"Come on, Viga. Come to bed. It's late for you too." My Father broke mom off mid-sentence. "I told you to butt out!" he screamed at her. "I tell her when to leave, not you! I'm not finished with her yet. Now you shut up and get out of here...NOW! March!"

Through the pain in my head and neck, and the ache in my backside from his kick, I watched mom leave the room. I knew I had a long night ahead, a long night of being berated, sworn at, accused and abused. I would be reminded what a horrible, ungrateful daughter I was, guilt-tripped, made to promise I'd never be a bad girl again. And when he'd finished reducing me to shreds and was finally feeling he had proved yet again that he was the all-powerful one who deserved no less than complete subservience, he would kindly forgive me and "prove his love" for me with sex.

As the sun began to rise on a Sunday morning when all the believers would be off to pray to a God who I felt had long ago forsaken me, aching from head to toe, I crawled into my bed. I had a massive throbbing lump at the base of my skull from the blow with the snowbrush, but the blow to my head hurt less than the blow to my heart and mind. Who was I kidding? I would never be free of my father. I would never marry John. It was time to do something about all this. I would give John back his ring and tell him to get out of my rotten and rotted life.

CHAPTER 36: BIRD WITH A BROKEN WING

That Sunday was a "fuzzy" day for me. I slept very late and on rising, the pain of the blow to my head seared through my skull. I felt slightly dizzy and nauseous. My father was walking around the house, whistling happily as if the night before had never happened. When I entered the kitchen, he was smiling and friendly, and commented on how awful I looked. I mentioned I was nauseous but he immediately suggested I had probably eaten and drunk too much at the party. I said nothing. He knew better than that. My mother just shot him a look of disgust that thankfully he didn't see as he took himself outside to shovel the snow, reminding me there was a second shovel for me in the garage to use as soon as I'd had something to eat!

Of course, I couldn't eat a thing. I sipped some tea, my head whirling with thoughts mingled with the pain. I looked at my mom.

"Mom...I can't go on like this! Dad is insane. He's a monster. His anger is out of control. If he keeps up like this, one day he's going to kill me."

Nausea got the better of me as I spoke and I ran to the bathroom to hurl. Oh, how my head and neck ached! When I got back to the kitchen, mom looked at me forlornly. I made her feel the throbbing lump at the base of my skull.

"My God! It's huge!" she said. "How did that get there?"

She hadn't seen him whack me with the snowbrush in the garage. I told her, seizing the opportunity to continue with an idea that had been on my mind since I got up.

"Mom...I need to go to the police about Dad. This is abuse. It's been going on for years and lately, it's getting worse. Last night was horrible. He was more violent than ever. You went to bed but he continued punching and hitting me as he lectured me on and on till sunrise."

I broke off on the point of telling her what else he'd done, how he'd then made me go down on him, bring him to orgasm, then started lecturing me some more to show me who's boss and how I shouldn't mess with him and how just before sunrise he'd mounted me again, pummeling me hard as if to drive the point home that I was his to do with as he wanted. I so wanted to tell her everything, but still I couldn't.

"Oh, Viga" mom said. "You wouldn't do that, would you? You can't go to the police about your own father! You can't!"

She looked incredulous at the suggestion. I felt my resolve faltering as she said:

"It's not that bad, is it? It's not like he beats you every day. He's not always like this ... "

I hesitated, again wanting to tell her everything, but I couldn't spit it out.

I tried again. "Mom, it's not about how often. What? Are you blind? Don't you see how mad he gets? He's out of control when he's in a rage. Last night, it was kicking and now I have a monster lump on my head. What will it be next time? Or maybe it will be you! He came close to hitting you too last night."

"He won't touch me," mom replied. "He hasn't hit me in years. He promised me he'd never hurt me again and I know one thing about him: he keeps his word!"

"Of course he doesn't hit you!" I nearly screamed in exasperation. "He's got me for his punching bag! You don't know the half of it! You're always off napping or sleeping. You don't see or hear what he says or does to me!"

Mom said nothing for a moment. She glanced out the window to see if he was still shoveling. "You know, you'd better get out there and help him before he gets mad again..."

I looked at her in disbelief. "Oh, so that's it. Just like that you're going to let go of what I was just saying?"

"Well, what do you want me to do?" she yelled back at me.

"I want you to support me! You're my mother. You see what's going on. You've even tried to stop him and you can't. I want to go to the police and I want you to come with me!"

Mom looked at me as if I'd struck her. "What? I could never do that! I could never report your Father to the police. He's not a criminal. He...he..."

I felt the resolve in me disappear. It was hopeless. She was hopeless. I was hopeless. Without her support, I was helpless, lost.

"So..." I said quietly, "so you won't help me?" I sighed. "Guess I'll go help him shovel snow," I mumbled as I walked out of the room. He'd won again.

I spent another night in pain and was just getting out of my morning shower when my Father, who was on afternoon shift, suddenly appeared in the doorway in his underwear. Mom had left for work an hour earlier. I was still feeling nauseous and my head was throbbing away.

"Got time for a quickie?" he asked.

I looked at the gargoylian leer as I'd come to see his "I want sex" look and felt the nausea starting in my gut again/

"Dad...I...I really feel kinda sick this morning. My stomach's not good at all and my head is throbbing from that whack..."

I broke off. We hadn't spoken of that since he hit me. He didn't even know about the lump. "Besides... I don't really have time. I have to be at school earlier on Mondays for weekly staff briefing before school starts."

"Phone in sick," he suggested, with just a hint of command.

"Oh dad, I can't do that! They'd have to get a supply teacher and there isn't time now to arrange one!"

"Bullshit!" he shouted. "You wake up sick on a morning and you call in sick. Period! They will find someone! Now call in sick!"

I started to protest again. I just couldn't bear the thought of him touching me this morning. Bile rose in my throat and I lurched for the toilet and heaved. As I wiped my mouth off, he said:

"Now what the fuck is this you're pulling? What, are you now trying to show me you really are too sick for me? Well, if you're too sick for me, you're too sick for work! Call in now!"

As I walked past him to go to the phone, his leg came up suddenly and landed a blow to my hip. I fell over, slamming my arm against the sofa. Before I could get up, his foot came down hard on my ear. Pain shot through my already aching head. I could barely move.

"Get up!" he shrieked. "Make that call! Now you really are too sick to go to work, right?"

I started crying and was so slow getting up, he grabbed my arms and pulled me up, pushing me toward the phone. "Why are you being so stubborn?" he yelled.

"What? Are you in such a hurry to see that fucking kangaroo?"

Oh, so that was it. Despite my not giving him any reason to think otherwise, at least not consciously, he was convinced something was going on. No wonder his brutality with me was escalating. He was using his last resort again, the one that had worked for years: my fear of him. And it worked again. I phoned in sick.

When I returned to work a day later, things did not go well. I was called into the principal's office to explain the late phone-in. Didn't I realize that was not acceptable? Didn't I know protocol? Did I not realize what an inconvenience I had caused since they couldn't arrange a supply on such short notice and other staff had had to cover my classes and I'd left no assignments and...! On and on the principal went and inwardly I shrunk into a shameful blob. I didn't need this just now and yes, I knew all that but she just didn't understand that it had all been out of my control.

Or had it? I was making excuses again for my own failure to act, my failure to stand up to my father, to go to the police with or without my mother's support or to tell John it was over and to get out of my life. I felt like that bird with a broken wing, wanting to fly, but with a broken wing, I lacked the courage to even try.

I could barely look at John when I saw him at lunch. I just wanted to close my eyes and pretend he wasn't there and I'd never met him. He kept asking me what was wrong, why I'd missed a day, was I better now? I kept dismissing his questions, dismissing him. My head still throbbed mercilessly and I begged his silence with a Greta Garbo "I just want to be alone" attitude, blaming it all on a bad headache. I dragged myself through classes, and dreaded returning home. When I gave John a quick, cool kiss goodbye, he look puzzled and sad.

"What's wrong, Viga? Tell me," he implored. "I'm not blind. This is more than a headache, isn't it. Something's changed. What is it?"

"It's nothing!" I snapped. "I just don't feel well!

Haven't you ever had a bad headache? I'm sorry. I have to go!"

"What's the rush? Why do you have to rush home every day!"

"I just do. That's all!" I responded almost coldly now. "You wouldn't understand."

I drove off before he could ask more. I didn't know how to tell him I was doing everything I could to push him out of my head, my heart, my life. Maybe if he fell out of love with me, he would end what I couldn't. I loved him too much to do it myself. I was a bird with a broken wing and a breaking heart.

Bird with broken wing
Wants to fly
Too scared to try

ODE TO AN URN

You walked across my brain last night
And we fought the same old fight
You telling me it was alright for a father
to molest his daughter

I told you NO It wasn't okay
Told you GO ... just go away
But you didn't, wouldn't
You stayed like you shouldn't
Last night and way back then

Why can't you just leave me alone?

You've been dead so many years
But my fears and tears continue to pour
Just like before
Suddenly jolting me from nightmare dreams
Making me fall apart at the seams
Spewing up memories I've tried so hard to erase:
Your touch, your smell, your face

What are you now? Just dust, bones, ash
Cremated remains I can't even trash
'Cause that's against the law

Against the law?

Well, so was what you did to me
And that is now the legacy
I carry in my soul and mind
And try as I may, I can't leave it behind

Even now when I go to bed at night
I hear you saying "It's alright"

But you know what daddy? It wasn't alright
And I still don't sleep very well at night.

©Viga Boland, March 2013

CHAPTER 37: D-DAY

As much as it annoys me sometimes, it's a good thing that my husband was never much good at reading between the lines or interpreting body language. If he were, he might have walked out of my life after that episode. I kept up my cold, "just go away" attitude toward him all week as I tried to send him an unspoken message: I was no good for him, didn't deserve him, and we had no future together. Short of giving him back the engagement ring, which I did stop wearing and which brought curious looks, but thankfully, no questions from my students, in my mind we were done.

But with a patience and love for me that has kept us married for over forty years now, John hung in there, waiting for the woman he was determined to marry to return to herself. And I did. Try as I could not to, I loved him too and couldn't let this chance for my own happiness go. So when John decided the time had come, as terrified as I was when I heard these words:

"Viga, it's time I met your father and formally asked for your hand in marriage... "

I agreed. I was panicking inside but I had run out of excuses for delaying this any longer. The school year was ending, summer break was coming, and to John, always a logical thinker, it just made perfect sense to get married as soon as school was over so we could have a long honeymoon traveling Canada during school vacation.

For John, the whole thing was simple: "I love you and want to spend the rest of my life with you. You love me, don't you? We've known each other over a year now. We're not kids. I'm nearly 30 for heavens sake! I don't want to waste more time waiting, scurrying around, not able to date because of something I don't understand or a father whom I've never met. I want to take you out, introduce you to my friends, enjoy good times with you freely and go where we want when we want as man and wife! So what's the problem here?"

"The problem IS my father, John..." I replied weakly. "You just have no idea. He terrifies me!"

John wasn't going to be put off yet again. "So, are

you going to spend your whole life being terrified of him? What are you so terrified of? Is he going to kill you or something because you want what every woman has a right to have: love marriage, children? Don't you want these things enough yourself? Don't you want these things with me as much as I want them with you?'"

"Yes...of course I do... " I responded feebly, unsure. "It's just...just...I'm scared... "

"Well I'm not!" John stated forcefully. "I know I've never met the man but he can't be that bad. What's he going to do? Kill me?" He was smiling as he said this. He pointed to his muscles. "See these? I'm ready for him!"

I smiled but it wasn't funny. John was making jokes, but to my mind, he wasn't seeing the gravity of the situation.

How could he? He didn't realize he wasn't about to simply ask a father if he could marry his daughter. He was about to do battle with a jealous, possessive man who believed this woman belonged to him. And yes, I did fear for his safety, for his, more than mine in this case. I really did believe my father could, and would kill him. I looked at him, searching for some other way to do this.

"Maybe we could just elope or something?" I suggested. That seemed an easy, simple solution to me. "We could just vanish and by the time my father figures out what happened, we'll be long gone?"

"And what would we live on, sleeping beauty? This isn't a fairy tale. What about our jobs, income, etc?" John laughed. "No, we have to do it this way."

"Well...when are you thinking of doing this then?" I asked, not really wanting to hear his answer.

"How's this coming Sunday? I'm free. Let's get it done! The sooner the better so we can start planning the wedding."

I nearly gagged. Panic welled up in me. It was Friday. I had no time to prepare myself, or mom. How was I going to do this? Should I just let John show up at the door? Should I tell my father beforehand? When? Tomorrow? On Sunday itself? I was in turmoil. My stomach was tying itself in knots already. Again, I was about to protest, tell John it's too soon, to give me more time, but I looked at him and saw there was no point. He was right. I knew it was now or never.

"Okay," I agreed with a courage I certainly didn't feel. "Come over about 2 o'clock. That'll give me time to prepare him beforehand. But please understand, anything could happen. Don't expect him to welcome you with open arms... "

"Don't worry, love," John said gently, happily. Again, he pointed to his muscles and grinning, said: "I've got these remember? And if I have to, I'll use them. You are worth fighting for."

The period bell rang. We both grabbed our books and headed toward our next class. John looked confident and happy as he strode down the hall away from me. I wished I felt as he did. I was dying a thousand deaths at the thought of what might happen in two days time.

That historical Sunday rose bright and sunny. My father was relaxed, easy-going and cheery as he ate his breakfast and asked if I was going to help him mow the lawn. I said I'd be out in a bit, and once he was outside, I turned to mom, fear in my eyes and heart and said dully:

"Mom, John is coming over here today at 2 o'clock to meet dad and ask permission to marry me."

Shocked, Mom dropped the plate she was wiping. Pieces of porcelain flew all over the floor and I rushed to help her pick them up. Neither of us spoke as I let my words sink in. I knew that like me, she was panicking, filled with ugly visions of what might happen in just a couple of hours from now. My head had been full of them since John and I had parted with his shouting a happy "See you Sunday" on Friday afternoon. I'd barely slept the last couple of nights, had no appetite, and was in a constant state of nausea.

"Are you serious?" Mom finally said. "He's coming... here?"

"Yes. Here! Where else?" I replied, almost impatient with what seemed a stupid question. I knew she was just in shock, in denial as she'd been most of her life. Her answer to everything was to go have a nap and sleep it off and hope it would all just go away. Trouble is, like with booze and drugs, nothing ever got resolved or accomplished that way. It just got postponed. And this time, there would be no further postponements. John would be here at 2pm. I tried to control my own urge to just go to sleep and pretend it wasn't going to happen. I was so tired, exhausted from two sleepless nights of worry but I forged on when she foolishly said:

"He can't...I mean...call him and tell him not to come. No...it's too soon...your father will kill him. He...he ... will kill you...he..."

"Mom! Stop!" I screamed at her. "Just stop! I'm not going to call him. This has to happen! You know it as well as I do and I'm not going to put it off any longer! But I need you to support me for once! For just this once in my life can you be my mother and support me? I can't keep living like this! What, you think I'm not scared? I'm bloody terrified, as I've been all my life! As you've been. This is not living! And if he's going to kill me, then let him. I can't take any more but I need you to be really strong this time and help me."

"What's all the shouting?"

I froze. My father stood in the back doorway, removing his gardening gloves and wiping his sweaty brow.

"Is something wrong?" he asked again. He was smiling, still cheery. "Such a beautiful day outside, but hot. I need a drink of water!"

He walked over to the tap, downed a glass of water and turned to look at us both.

"Ahhhh..." he sighed, suddenly puzzled by the looks on our faces. Neither mom nor I had moved. We were frozen in fear.

"What's the matter with you two? You look like you've seen a ghost. What's up?" He turned to me. "I thought you were coming out to help me mow the lawn. Are you not feeling well or something?"

I looked at mom. Her eyes were wide with fear but they were urging me to speak up and speak up now. This was my chance. I knew I had better tell him before John arrived. Prepare him.

In a flash, as if I were watching a movie, I saw him flying into a rage, stabbing me, blood flying everywhere, my mother rushing to stop him and getting stabbed too, and then I saw him stabbing himself. In the same flash, I saw John arriving, taking in the scene, and running from the house to get help, all too late. It was all so dramatic, I almost started to laugh, but instead I looked at my father and tears began pouring down my face.

"Oh my goodness," said my father, "What's all this? If you don't feel like mowing the lawn, it's okay. Nothing to cry about."

I did start to laugh then, a nervous mixture of laughter and sobs that wouldn't stop coming from the deepest part of my soul. Years of pent up tears and fears poured down my face, punctuated by uncontrollable, hysterical laughter. Completely terrified, completely hysterical, anticipating the fury and bloodbath I was sure would follow, I blurted:

"This is not about the lawn or wanting or not wanting to mow it! It's about John and me...that f-ing kangaroo you keep asking about. He's coming over here in an hour's time to meet you! To ask your permission to marry me!"

Now it was my father's turn to look shocked. He turned slightly pale, looked quickly at mom in disbelief but surprisingly not in anger either, and asked her:

"Is this true? Did you know about it?"

"No...I didn't know..." said mom hesitantly. "She just told me now before you came in. That's what the shouting was about."

My father looked incredulous at what he'd just learned. I could tell he didn't quite believe her, but he was too shocked to question her further. He turned back to me, still blubbering away, waiting for his rage to start and bracing myself for the blows I was sure would follow. His next few words stunned me:

"Well...this is a surprise. I certainly wasn't expecting this when I got up today. Well, what can I say? I'm happy for you."

He took a breath, letting that sink in before adding in a voice that sounded dazed at what he'd just learned:

"He actually wants to marry YOU?"

I was still trying to recover from the shock of hearing him say he was happy for me, when I began to wonder at his emphasis on the word "you". Why was it so hard for him to believe someone might actually want to marry me? Did he really think I was that ugly or unlovable?

That hurt, but it stopped me from crying. With amazing self-control, I said:

"Yes, he wants to marry ME!"

"Well then..." he said slowly, "and do you want to marry him? Do you love him?"

"I do"

"Well how do you know if you love him? You kept saying you never see each other, never talk. You can't just marry someone you hardly know. You need time to get to know each other. When did you plan for this to happen?"

I couldn't believe he was actually saying all this. What was this? Was the bashing about to start? Was he beginning to work himself up into a rage? He couldn't be taking it this well, could he? This was too easy. I shifted uncomfortably, expecting him to explode with anger any minute, but answered his questions bravely.

"We haven't really set a date or anything yet. That's why he's coming over to talk to you." I glanced at the clock. "In fact, he'll be here very soon: 2 o'clock."

"Well then I better get myself cleaned up a bit. Mama put on a cuppa for me, will you?" My father turned to me. "And you better go wash your face a bit from all those tears. You don't look very good. Comb your hair too. I guess you want to look good when he arrives, right?"

Mama smiled hesitantly, warily. I headed for the bathroom in a bit of daze. This couldn't be happening, not so easily. Suddenly I was filled with fear. My stomach turned. Of course! He was saving his rage for John! Oh dear God! What would he do! What was he planning?

At 2 o'clock on the dot, John rang the doorbell. I was paralyzed with fear, almost willing him to disappear and me with him. My father had said very little as he sat there sipping coffee, but now he insisted on opening the door. I gulped, but followed him, ready to scream "Run!" to John if I thought my father was about to punch him. Instead, I watched wide-eyed with amazement as my father opened the door, smiled broadly at John and pleasantly invited him inside. It was all so "normal" it was abnormal!

What was going on with my father? Had I been asleep all those years since he first started abusing me and was just waking up from a nightmare? This wasn't the monster under and in my bed. This was a nice, ordinary everyday dad!

John stepped inside, shot me a puzzled but loving look, and shook hands with my father who was oozing goodwill and camaraderie. My father offered him a drink, poured them both a whiskey, and as they clicked glasses like two old friends who'd just bumped into each other after years apart, I looked at my mother. Like me, she looked stunned, shocked at what she was seeing. She quickly grabbed a glass for herself, asking me by actions if I wanted a drink too. I nodded a dazed "yes" but asked her to make mine a vodka and orange. No stinking whiskey for me, or the nightmare might resurface.

With all of us relaxing over a drink, my father plied John with questions about Australia, why he had come to Canada, how he liked it here, whether he planned to return home and when etc., etc. Mom and I said very little, too afraid to break the pleasant spell, too sure it could snap any second and all hell would break loose.

Every so often John would shoot me a questioning look that said he didn't really get what was happening here. Why had I been so afraid of this meeting? Why had he had to sneak around with me for months? My dad was just an ordinary, nice guy.

As my father poured each of them another drink, he turned to mom and said:

"Where are your manners mama? Put on some food. After all we had an important guest, my future son-in-law, and we need to feed him!"

Again, my jaw nearly hit the floor in shock. Where was Mr. Hyde hiding and when would he surface?

"So, when are you two thinking of having this wedding?" my father asked us both pleasantly. "After all, we may need some time to get the money together to finance this. Weddings aren't cheap."

I decided to finally speak up, very cautiously. "Well...John had suggested it would be nice to have a summer wedding since we get two months off from school?"

"So, you're thinking next summer then? A year from now? After all, you two need some more time to get to know each other, don't you agree? And, like I said, mama and I need to put some more money aside for this."

"Well, actually," John replied, comfortable now that all was going as it should, "I was hoping we could make it this summer. I think Viga and I know each other well enough by now to know what we feel is real. We love each other and I can't wait to call her my wife. I don't care about having a big wedding. We don't need to spend a ton of money. All I ask of you is your blessing and approval."

As he said this, John looked earnestly and openly at my father, before reaching across the kitchen table to squeeze my hand. His eyes were so full of love I just melted. He looked so handsome, so assured, so much the kind of husband any loving parents would want for their daughter. I glanced quickly at my father. His eyes were unreadable, his demeanor still pleasant and friendly.

"Okay. So I can see you two really are in love. Well, what can I say then but...welcome to the family, John!"

On that note, both John and my father stood up and hugged each other. My father actually did the European thing of kissing John on both cheeks which again shocked the rest of us. Mama and I jumped up and hugged and kissed my father simultaneously, showing our appreciation as he'd taught us to do for years, and we briefly hugged and kissed John too. I wanted to smother John in kisses but that little voice inside me warned me not to push my luck: it knew Mr. Hyde was never far from Dr. Jekyll. Despite all the warmth and goodwill my Father was showing us all now, experience had taught me to be forever vigilant. It couldn't possibly be this easy.

CHAPTER 38: THE CALM BEFORE THE STORM

It's hard to remember much more of that day now, not just because it all took place over forty-four years ago, but because of the almost surreal atmosphere surrounding it. Though not comparable in significance, it was like watching the events of 911 as they occurred: surreal...so horrific I couldn't believe my eyes. This, while not horrific, was equally unbelievable, even disorienting to me. I not only don't remember much more of that day or how it ended, but I don't remember much of the week that followed, apart from John saying to me at school the next morning how shocked he was by my Father's reaction and pleasant acceptance of him and the news we shared. I'd like a dollar for each time he said something akin to:

"I went into this expecting to meet and go into battle with an ogre and instead I met a really nice father... who actually kissed me for heavens sake! I just don't get it!"

Well neither did I and I actually felt a little stupid. Again, I began to wonder if I'd been asleep and having a nightmare all those years and had just now woken up or what? Had I created the monster I saw my father as? Had I imagined the years of mental, physical and sexual abuse? Even today as I write this, I've had to stop many times and ask myself if this or that really happened.

And yet somewhere deep inside me, I believe there's a lot that I've buried so deeply only therapy might dig it back up. But quite honestly, at this point in my life, that could prove catastrophic, given how a later session of hypnosis performed by my doctor for a headache, sent me so low I couldn't stop crying for hours after, and I didn't know why! I so badly frightened the doctor and my husband who was in the room at the time that I never dared try hypnosis again. Where had it taken me? I'm not sure I want to know.

What I do remember about the week that followed was a strange quietness that took over my father. He'd go to work, come home looking weary, even slightly defeated, but not angry. Mom and I continued to walk and talk warily around him, even touching a bit on the pending wedding within earshot of him, but still he said little. He'd even ask after John, then retire to his TV and that despised chesterfield. To my relief, he also never indicated I should join him there. For the first time in twelve years, he didn't force sex on me. That felt wonderful, doubly so because after I'd fallen in love with John, my sense of shame, guilt and dirtiness had increased ten-fold. How could it not? I felt guilty about my father when I was with John but I felt even guiltier and filthier when I was with my father.

As this week, a historical one for me, drew to a close, I felt a great tension rising inside me. My father's strange silence was part of the reason: it felt like the calm before the storm. The other reason for the tension was I was about to test my father's true feelings about my changed status from that of his "mistress" to another man's fiancée.

A year-end staff party was being thrown on that Friday night by one of the female staff. Naturally, I wanted to go: this would be my first non-secret date with John and it was both exciting and important to me. John planned to pick me up around 7pm. Shortly after my father arrived home and parked himself in front of the TV, I brought him some hot tea, and not without some fear, said to him as I handed him the mug:

"Dad, there's a year-end staff party tonight being thrown by one of the girls. Do you have any objection to my going?"

He turned his clear blue eyes on me and fear shot through me like an arrow. His eyes were cold, angry. I knew that look too well. Suddenly the full mug of tea was being hurled at my face. I felt a hot splash and heard the mug crashing against the wall behind me.

"And what the fuck are you asking me for?" he screamed at me. "What the fuck do you care what I think? All these months you've been lying to me, cheating on me, fucking that kangaroo then coming home and fucking me after him you, bloody whore! I told you I hate liars! I hate cheats! To think he was having you while I was having you...Ugh! You disgust me, you filthy cunt! Dirty, filthy cunt! Get out of my sight!"

"Dad...dad..." I protested weakly. "It wasn't like that at all, not at all! John hasn't touched me! I love you

Daddy, but I want a normal life. I'm 23. I want a ring on my finger, a husband, children..."

As I spoke, his face turned redder and redder with rage. The volcano had been brewing all week. Now it was erupting.

"Don't give me that! What do you take me for? Some idiot? Some jelly-livered weakling? No woman tells me what to do! No woman tells me what she wants! Babies? You want babies? I could have given you one of those! You want a ring? I gave you one of those already..."

It was true. He had come home one day months prior with two beautiful diamond rings he'd bought from some guy at work. He'd given one to mom in a big display of affection. The other he had shown to me privately, told me it was my wedding ring from him. He said we had to keep it hidden but I should consider myself married... to him!

"Dad ... dad!" I tried again to calm him down. "Dad, you know you can't really do all that. You have a wife. I am your DAUGHTER, your daughter... not your wife!"

He turned furious eyes on me now. He was wild with rage, hurt, love and hate.

"Daughter?" He hissed. "You are not my daughter! No daughter would treat her father as you have treated me!" His voice softened, broke. I saw tears spring to his eyes.

"I loved you! You don't know how much I loved you! I loved you more than any father could love a daughter. More than any man could love a woman. And this...this..."

He broke off for a second, wiped away a tear almost in self-disgust at showing his own pain so much, and I watched and heard as the rage replaced his hurt yet again:

"And this," he continued, "is how you repay me? Get out of my sight!" he screamed. "Get out! Get out! You are not my daughter! You are nothing but a fucking whore and I don't want another fucking whore in my house. I married one of those! Now get out of my sight before I kill you, fucking cunt! Pack your bags! Go to your party with your fucking kangaroo! Get out of here in half an hour and if you're not out of here in half an hour I'll throw you out! Get out! Now! Go!"

I flew out of the room, and ran into the kitchen. My mom was standing there biting her lip nervously and wringing her hands together.

"Mom...Mom... what do I do? He's gone nuts!"

"You do what he said!" she replied as calmly as she could in a voice that was shaking. "Pack up what you can as fast as you can and get out!"

"But I've got nowhere to go! Nowhere to live..."

"You and John will figure something out. Just get out now. This is what you wanted. He's given it to you. Now take it and hurry up before he comes out here or you may never get out of here!"

Crying, I ran into my bedroom and started grabbing anything and everything. I have no idea what I took, probably mainly whatever was needed for school and some clothes and shoes. I was running, packing frantically, box after box that mom dug up hurriedly from the basement. At some point my father stepped into the living room where he could see me piling up boxes. I was sobbing uncontrollably, not really knowing or seeing what I was doing. But my father's wrath was unabated. He was still furious.

"Go on!" he taunted. "Hurry up. Your half-hour is almost up!" He grabbed a framed photo of me from the wall and flung it at me. The frame broke; glass shattered. He picked it up, tore the photo from the frame, ripped it to shreds, and threw the pieces at my tear-streaked, frightened face.

"That is what I think of you and your tears" he shrieked, "you false, lying cunt! You are nothing to me! You don't exist for me! Get out of my life! Don't ever show your lying face here again!"

He turned on his heel and disappeared just as John pulled into the driveway. I ran out to him before he could ring the doorbell. I was terrified my father would come at him. One look at me wiped the smile off John's face.

"Good God! What's happened? Why are you crying?" He asked.

"Don't ask me now!" I nearly screamed. "Just get this stuff into your car and get us out of here!"

John and I loaded the car haphazardly going as fast as we could. I looked at mom. She was white with fear. I went to hug her her but she said:

"GO! Don't waste time now! Just GO!"

"Will you be alright mom?" I hesitated. Knowing my father's fury, I was afraid to leave her with him. What if he took his rage out on her.

"I'll be okay!" she insisted urgently. "Just get out of here...now...before he comes back and sees John. Please... I'll be fine. He won't touch me. GO!"

With one last look at the mother I loved but never really knew, I got into John's little car and we drove away from the life I'd known and hated for the last twelve or so years. I felt so strange: I was free at last, but not free of years of painful, dirty memories, shame, and self- loathing. I was moving away from a life that though hated, was familiar, and moving into a life that was unknown, scary. And I was riddled with guilt: for the umpteenth time, I felt like everything was my fault!

I could see my father's face twisted in a weird mixture of love and hate, weeping tears I'd never before seen come from him. Somehow, that made me feel so bad, even selfish. And I could see poor little mom's face, pale but brave, ready to face what I knew would be hurled at and dumped on her now. My fear for her was greater than my fear for myself. In his anger, what might he do to her now? Would he take out his rage at me on her? After all these years of silence, mom had finally shown me the love I didn't think she had for me and I'd left her to deal with him. I was consumed with guilt at what I'd done.

Lost in tumultuous thoughts, while tears continued to pour down my face and my body shook between sobs, I almost forgot where I was, where we were going, or that John was even with me until his hand slid over to grasp mine.

"Are you going to be okay?" He asked gently, afraid to probe, but needing to know where I was at. "Should we still go to this party?"

I wiped away my tears and desperately searched my purse for tissues to blow my nose. John pulled a handkerchief out of his pocket.

"Want to use this? It's clean. Fresh out of the wash... " For some reason I found that terribly funny. I didn'tknow people still used hankies, somehow so passé.

I began to laugh uncontrollably, almost hysterically as years of bottled-up emotions toppled over each other and spilled down my face in a mixture of laughter and tears.

It would be the first time of many that John would see me as a confusing, emotional basket-case, but not always for sad reasons. Eleven years later he would see me laughing and crying all at once, but this time with joy as I looked down at the beautiful pink face of our beloved firstborn daughter, Kim. And then again, eighteen months later, when I held our second beautiful daughter, Victoria, swaddled in green hospital towels. I would laugh and cry simultaneously in the joyous knowledge, albeit subconscious, that with a father like John, neither of my daughters would suffer as I had in a father's hands.

I emptied my dripping nose into John's hanky and looked embarrassedly at him, not knowing what to do with it. He looked at me and grinned.

"Well...I don't really want it back just now," he laughed.

I laughed with him. I suddenly felt good, relieved. I had done it! I was out of that house, away from a life I never wanted, asked for, nor deserved. In one way at least, I was free of my father at last. Now all I had to do was put all the bad memories, the guilt, the shame where they belonged: the garbage. That wouldn't be easy. It would take years, over forty in fact, but I had just closed a door and walked through a new one. My heart filled with hope for a brighter tomorrow.

"So...what do you want to do?" John asked me again.

"Let's get drunk and celebrate my freedom!" I said. "Let's party!"

IT'S NOT OVER

Music, Lyrics ©Andrew Rudd, Victoria Boland 2010

I'd been down deeper than I'd even been
I was drowning underneath my sea of tears
I was out further than an angel's reach
I was incomplete losing to my fears

I was ashamed cornered by the things I felt
Feeling jaded by the ones who'd let me down
Where could I go? I was lost within my labyrinth
I was frightened of the life I didn't know
But then you came along, you held out your hand
You brushed off my cheeks and made me understand

That there's more to life when you close a door
And if the road just ends
you turn around and start to search for more
You sometimes have to bend and learn how to forgive
And when the world is on your shoulders... It's not over

I was blamed; they said it all had been intentional
They called me selfish not admitting to their faults
But it was right, doing what I had to do
It hurt me deeply more than they could ever know
But you said to be strong and yet you still let me cry
Stood by me each day and said all good things take time

'Cause there's more to life when you close a door
And if the road just ends you turn around and start to
search for more
You sometimes have to bend and learn how to forgive
And when the world is on your shoulders...It's not over

From the CD, **"AndrewVictoria"** available from
http://www.andrewvictoria.com

CHAPTER 39. ON MY OWN BUT NOT ALONE

The next couple of weeks were traumatic. For the first time in my life I was on my own, though not alone. It all felt so strange. I felt empowered but insecure, experienced but naive, liberated but lost.

This was 1971 and living together, even if engaged, wasn't what nice girls did. John had been raised in a very Catholic family: he still attended Sunday Mass and for me to move in with him, though tempting, was somehow sinful. And besides, the two of us could never fit in the tiny single bed in his basement apartment!

So I rented a pokey room in a rooming house with a single set of rickety drawers and the lumpiest bed ever. The other tenants, by my father's standards, were the low-life's of this world: waitresses, factory floor-sweepers, divorcees...folks who lived from pay-cheque to pay-cheque when they could get a job or keep one long enough to buy the next bottle of plonk or pack of cigarettes. It was eye opening for me to mix with people like this, so different from my family's circle of friends or even my fellow staff-mates.

It was simultaneously scary and exciting for me to live temporarily with this group, scary because I kept envisioning one of the drunken men coming into my room to try and have their way with me, but exciting because of finally having the freedom to come and go as I pleased. That was such a new experience and with every day, I liked it more and more: no longer having to ask a man for permission to go here or go there, to do this or do that! I could wear what clothes I wanted, experiment with makeup and leave it on, choose what to do with my time when I wasn't teaching or with John planning the wedding. The freedom was exhilarating! The teenager I was never allowed to be resurfaced. I was almost as giddy as the Grade 9 and 10's I was teaching, even feeling like one of them at times, understanding instead of disapproving their silliness and youthful exuberance. For the first time since that day my father decided to educate me about men, I felt almost normal.

And yet, as I tossed about on that lumpy mattress

at night, I battled guilt: I felt guilty about the chaos I had caused my parents; I felt guilty about leaving mom alone to clean up the debris of the storm I had rained down on their lives; and I felt guilty about the misgivings I was having about marrying a man I truly barely knew!

John and I had had anything but a normal courtship. We'd never really dated. Our times together had been stolen moments in his car, a quick grabbed lunch at a local hot food place, a movie with mom tagging along, a short but lovely trip to Niagara Falls on icy roads that nearly landed us in a ditch, or furtive cuddles on an old mattress in our basement while mom kept nervous watch at the window upstairs. What did I know about this man I was about to marry? I'd never met his family. He talked non-stop about returning to his beloved Australia, a thought that terrified me. His greatest passions were cars, aircraft and photography, all of which meant little to me, and he had no interest in live theatre, musicals, writing poetry or the pursuits I enjoyed. How could we possibly build a life together when we didn't really have that much in common?

I truly began to question what I had done. Would I end up wrecking John's life too? And what of myself? I'd spent twenty-three years dominated by a man. Now, I finally had a taste of what it was like to be on my own, answering to no-one but myself. Was I now so quickly going to give that expensively acquired freedom away and once again have to answer to a male for the rest of my life? I tossed and turned on that lumpy mattress suddenly wishing I could just disappear to explore my freedom more fully, more deeply and most importantly, to find that teenager who was buried beneath the dirt in those nightmares that had plagued me through so many years of abuse.

CHAPTER 40. LOVE CONQUERS ALL

In the end, that famous adage, 'Love Conquers All" proved true. Despite my misgivings about marrying John and giving up my newly acquired freedom, my love for him won out. We set the wedding date for July 3rd, immediately after school ended for the year and before everyone took off for summer vacation.

Money was very tight. I had none. My pay was still being automatically deposited in the mutually shared family account my father had set up, and he had told my mother to tell me I was not to touch the one lump cheque that came at school end or they wouldn't be able to make the mortgage payment that month. Dutiful, obedient and still terrified daughter that I was, I agreed.

As a result, John paid my rent and all the costs we were accumulating for the wedding. Of course, without any parental support, we financed the wedding as cheaply as possible, handwriting invitations on store-bought stationery and booking the least expensive restaurant facilities we could find that would allow us to supply our own alcohol. And when it came to our wedding attire, John rented the most affordable ordinary black tuxes available for himself and two groomsmen, while my maid of honor used a dress from a previous wedding and borrowed the matching one for my other bridesmaid.

As for my wedding dress, well there was no way I could shop for it without John: he was paying for it. We hit one of the big wedding dress clearance centers in Toronto and considered ourselves lucky indeed to purchase a very simple gown for a whole $25! I found some plain netting in Fabricland along with a $2 rhinestone headband and hand-stitched the netting to it. The result was lop-sided but on the big day, no-one noticed, or if they did, said nothing. In John's eyes I looked beautiful and that was all that mattered.

Given the circumstances, our wedding day went as well as, or even better than I could have hoped. After all, the two most important people in my life on that day were there, the first being my Mother.

It was hard for me to be walked down the aisle by

one of my father's best friends...Frank...that same Frank who had questioned my father's control over my life in the past. My father never forgave Frank for doing so... but if my father had stopped my little mom from attending, I would have been devastated. I don't even know how she got to the wedding (she didn't drive at the time) but I learned many years later of the verbal and mental abuse she copped from my father for standing up to him when he insisted she "be a good wife for once in her life and stand by her husband" and not attend the wedding.

Throughout all the smiles and good wishes and chatter of the day, many times I caught her sad, frightened eyes watching us. I tried not to think about what she would face when she finally got home from the wedding. And from what she later said, it was awful: my Father had spent the entire day, and the two weeks prior, alternating between rages and tears, one minute cursing her, then cursing me and threatening to take a gun and shoot me as I came down the aisle to breaking down into a crying, useless mess of a man betrayed and abandoned by the woman he saw as his wife.

How terribly hard it must have been for my mother to put up with this, never fully understanding why he felt this way about his daughter. My mother said it was many, many months before his mood swings abated and she stopped hearing about how I had taken away his reason for living when I chose another man over him.

"How false she was!" he complained to mom. "So false! Always singing that song "As long as he needs me, I know just where I'll be." She knew where she'd be alright! With him...not with me! But she let me believe she'd always be with me."

"Bogdan, she was just singing the song because you liked it and asked her to sing it. She didn't put a meaning to it. You did. Anyway, how long did you expect her to live at home with us?"

The other person who mattered most to me on that day and attended the wedding was John. Now why would I make a point of that here when, after all, he was the groom! Well, everyone has heard stories of brides being abandoned at the altar, right? According to John's best man, if it weren't for him and his wife, John would have been in a plane flying back to Australia on our wedding day if they hadn't just about tied him to chair and stood watch over him during the twenty-four hours before the wedding!

That's right: my wonderful husband developed cold feet. Just as I was unsure about taking this life-changing step, so was he. Not that anyone could blame him! What did he really know about me? What kind of crazy family was he marrying into? Would he ever be able to have a normal relationship with his in-laws? And from what he'd now learned about my Father's temper, would he, or I, ever be safe in my Father's presence should we one day run into him or even reconcile? Just what kind of load was he taking on here? In retrospect, I think if John had known the true story of what had gone on in my Father's home for the past twelve years, I might indeed have been left stranded at the altar!

In our photo archives of that wedding is a slide. It shows a very sheepish-looking John standing with his best man, Dennis, near the altar, waiting for his bride to start her walk up the aisle toward him. It's a funny picture and the look on his face cracks us both up. He looks stunned, scared. You can almost hear his thoughts shouting: "What the hell am I doing here? Get me out of here quick!" And as he's occasionally jokingly said over the past forty plus years of marriage,

"All I needed was one negative word from Dennis for me to say I'm out of here! But then, suddenly there you were, my bride, soon to be my wife, coming up the aisle and you looked so beautiful. In the instant that Frank handed you over to me and I took my rightful place beside you, all the doubts vanished. Beside you was where I belonged... forever."

As I walked up the aisle, I was trembling. My entire body was shaking with emotion and years of pent-up fears and tears, both for the past and to some degree, for the future. But as Frank passed me over to John, and my handsome groom took my hand, winked and whispered to me:

"Hi ya, kiddo!"

I too knew I was at last where I belonged. I proudly took my position, this time beside the right man...till death do us part.

JULY 3, 1971

AFTERMATH and AFTERTHOUGHTS:

As of July 3rd, 2013, John and I will have been married 42 years. By today's standards, we are marital dinosaurs. But when we promised ourselves to each other, we meant it.

It hasn't been easy to stay together over 42 years. We've had many ups and downs, moved houses seven to ten times, and even countries twice. We were in business together for many of those years. Cross-continent moves and being in business together 24/7 can really test a marriage! And during it all, the battle with my father, no longer just my battle, cast its pall over our own little family and tested our love for each other even more.

We eventually "reconciled" with my father about three years after the wedding, but a normal relationship between my father and his son-in-law was never really possible. Family get-togethers were often tension-filled, with my father suddenly exploding over any comment he didn't like. His face would redden in rage and he'd abruptly tell mom to, "Move! We're leaving!" No amount of apologizing nor asking him to calm down would work. With mom meekly in tow, he'd barge out the door telling me (ever weak in the presence of his anger) that I was okay but he didn't have to put up with that rude husband of mine! Shaken and crying, I'd close the door behind them and look at poor John, still sitting at the table over a half-eaten dinner I'd taken so much care to prepare, wondering what the hell he'd done or said wrong this time. I'd feel so bad that he too was a victim of my father's selfishness, narcissism and infinite need to have everyone cater to his wishes. John never really knew why he was so despised.

Even when my beloved daughters were born (we were childless by choice for nine years) family get-togethers were far from joyous. While my mom gushed over and loved her grandchildren madly, and lived for the chance to come visit for a few days, she often returned home to an angry, surly grandfather who derided her for wanting to spend time with us instead of with him! He guilt-tripped her terribly the few times a year she asked permission to stay with us for a few days, playing the martyr left alone to cook and care for himself. And when the girls were older, we all steeled ourselves for that monthly trip to the grandparents, silently praying the visit would go smoothly. It was almost funny to hear us all letting out a collective sigh of relief as we waved goodbye when the visit went without incident for a change.

Though both John and my daughters could never quite understand why things weren't easy and "normal" with my parents, and often asked, I revealed nothing about what had gone on in my home before our marriage. In fact, I never told my husband or my girls any of my story until I was in my early 60's, by which time both my parents had died. Yes, it took that long to finally find the courage to share what I considered the excrement of my earlier life. Like those nightmares I'd begun having immediately after my father embarked on years of violating his daughter, I always felt like I was walking around covered in excrement that no amount of toilet paper could wipe off and that everyone could see. Even now, though I've finally come out from under my dirty, shameful secret, I don't feel squeaky clean. Will I ever?

But despite that, since getting away from my father's stranglehold on my mind, body and soul, bit by bit and with the freedom of having a loving husband who has allowed me to be me, I've grown and achieved so much. I've taken on career challenges, blown a few and succeeded beyond my own expectations with others. With each success, my confidence has risen just that much more, but my past, the pain, the suffering and the shame, has kept me humble. As I said way back in the beginning when I talked about Desi and the toast or Mrs. Nastrom's curio cabinet, I learned very early that I can't always have what I want. Those early lessons were good preparation for life. I pity those children who are given everything they want and never have to work for them: suffering and hardship, if it doesn't kill us, makes us stronger, at least mentally.

And then there's my mother's role in all this. Every year when Mother's Day rolls around, I think of her, now dead seven years. How did she, wittingly or unwittingly contribute to my abuse?

For years I believed she knew nothing of the abuse, but today, after listening to so many victims of incest who have almost as much anger toward their mothers as they do their abusers, I have to ask myself was I too, simply in denial about my mother, just as she was in denial about my father and what was going on? I have sadly concluded "yes", Mama knew. But she spent all those years telling herself what she suspected just couldn't be happening.

It didn't help that not once in all those years did I tell her any of it. I just couldn't. I was so ashamed, I couldn't tell my mother or ask for her help. Also, as is obvious from what I've related in this story, my father had such incredible control over my thinking that he'd convinced me from the beginning that telling mom, or anyone, was futile: no-one would believe me. He had also kept my mouth shut by assuring me he'd deny it all, saying I'd dreamt it up or worse yet, telling them I wanted it. And from what mom told me before she died, he had indeed told her it was all my idea, that he'd just given me what I asked for. I was floored when my mother told me this, not so much that he told her that...that was just like him...but that sadly, she had believed him. That broke my heart.

But it certainly explained why when she came to

live with us, which she did till she died, she was almost hostile toward me and even John. My father had completely brainwashed her against us in the years following my leaving home. He'd convinced her we would never care for her as he did; that given the chance, we would take all her money and abandon her. She even had friends showing her nice retirement homes and would taunt me saying she had the money to set herself up nicely in one. Being as sensitive as I am, I often felt her friends didn't like me, were cautious in my presence, and felt I didn't care for my mother as much as they did. I once asked her what she was telling them about me and she'd say "Nothing!" But I saw the looks on their faces, and now, so many years later, I know she was lying. She couldn't be honest with them or me. Worse yet, she couldn't be honest with herself, just as she hadn't been honest with herself all those years.

But despite that, despite what she believed about me, thanks to my father, I never abandoned her and looked after her till the moment of her passing. As I watched the grey pallor of death on her face and waited out the long intervals between each dying breath on that hospital bed, I took her little feet in my hands and kissed them and told her how much I had always loved her, a little mouse of a woman who had lived a life of denial in denial.

As for my father, we were all there for him too in his final days. Cancer had ravaged his body quickly over a period of several months. He was little more than a skeleton his last few days. He refused a hospital or doctors, and even in the last few hours was still barking orders at my mother and calling her names as she rushed to clean up the pee when he missed the toilet.

One of my own proudest moments as a mother was seeing how my elder daughter, Kim, took control as he lay dying, ministering his morphine and wiping his brow. It was more love and care than I felt he deserved. She was doing for him what I couldn't bring myself to do. All I could think was soon the nightmare of my life would be over. No more would my family have to suffer through his rages and tirades. No more would we all have to bite our tongues instead of saying what was really on our minds. No more would we all have to cater, bow and apologize to him for imagined wrongs. No more would I have to hear him say how mom was the one woman who truly loved him and stood by him all those years when I and everyone else turned our backs on him ... and then turn around and curse her and call her names in the next breath. As he lay dying, instead of feeling sad, I was full of anticipation. I was anticipating my final release from the shackles he had put on me fifty or so years earlier.

My father was craving all sorts of food in those final hours and we were running around trying to satisfy each demand, when he suddenly took his last gasp with none of us in the room. In hindsight, that was strangely fitting. I returned from buying hot fries to see mom in tears, sobbing with guilt that she'd not been in the room when she heard him gasping for air.

I looked at Kim for confirmation: was he truly gone? She nodded. Slowly I walked into the room and went to his bedside.

He looked peaceful, silent at last. I touched his face. I lifted up his hand and felt the cooling fingers. And I felt nothing. Nothing. My mind wandered back to my wedding day, what mom had said about how he had cried all day. Why was he crying? Who was he crying for? Obviously for himself, for what he had lost. He had once told me that if you love something or someone, you set it free, even if it breaks your heart. He had told me that was how much he loved me, and in his mind, he had proved it. I almost felt sorry for him then as the vision of him crying over losing me on my wedding day crossed my mind. Or was I still simply guilt-tripping yet again?

Now, the once all powerful, controlling, Mr. Hyde lay there, no longer breathing, no longer teaching, preaching, manipulating everything and everyone around him. He was no longer capable of hurting anyone. But he had loved me in his own warped way. It was a love I could never understand. And as much as it shames me to say it, I loved him too, but who I loved was the dad I lost when I was eleven.

And now, as a result, I felt nothing. Not sad. Not sorry for him. Not even relieved for myself. Nothing.

I spoke to him, knowing now he couldn't hear me, hit me, tell me what to think or hurt me ever again. I asked him a simple question to which I knew there would never be an answer:

"Why? Why couldn't you have just been my dad?"

I would have cried for my dad, but I had no tears for this dead man on the bed who had told me once too often:

"You are not my daughter!"

Those words, and so many of his others that had hurt me so much over the years had emptied me of tears. Now, as he lay there dead, I had no tears for my father.

NO TEARS FOR MY FATHER

There were no tears for my father
On the day he chose to die
There was no-one in the room
To even say good-bye

He picked the perfect moment
He timed it very well
To take his leave of life
And free us from his hell

And I tried to find some sadness
Tears somewhere deep inside
But the well had emptied long before
The day my father died

©*Viga Boland, 2013*

ABOUT MY MOTHER:

Just about everyone who reads this book asks about my mother's role in my situation. Did she enable it? Did she know? Why didn't she do something? Some readers have said they came to hate my mother. I didn't. I see her as much a victim as I was. I don't forgive my father, but I do forgive my mother. My follow-up memoir, **"Learning to Love Myself"** tells you why I loved her then and always will. Read an excerpt from that book at the end of this book. The poem below is what I think she'd tell you:

People always ask her
Didn't your mother know?
I'd like to answer for her
But I died so long ago

I died the day he took me
And filled me with her life
I died again inside the church
When I became his wife

I died each time he punched me
And told me to obey
Reminding me of vows I made
On our wedding day

I died when he called me stupid
And said I had no brain
I died because he was heartless
And cared nothing 'bout my pain

I died each time he hit her
Hating how weak I'd become
But when you're dying inside
You can't help anyone

I was dead by the time he took her
And the dead no longer see
Entombed in a coffin of denial
A ghost as she become another me

© *Viga Boland 2015*

DEAR READER

Dear Reader and fellow victim/survivor of incest:

Oprah Winfrey once said:

"What I know for sure is this: You are built not to shrink down to less, but to blossom into more. To be more splendid. To be more extraordinary. To use every moment to fill yourself up."

It is nearly impossible to fulfill that vision as long as we believe and live with what our abusers told us about ourselves. The words with which they manipulated us for their own pleasure influence everything we are, think and do, even years after their abuse has stopped. (See poem "Who Am I?")

From my perspective, the abuse inflicted on my body by my father is nothing compared to the damage he did to my mind, my self-esteem and my self-love, and it's taken years of love and support from my family and a heck of a lot of self-talk to make me feel good about myself again. I now know I was put on this earth for something bigger and better than to satisfy my father's demands … that I was meant to "blossom into more" become "more splendid" and "more extraordinary".

I also know and believe with all my heart that none of us can become more extraordinary or more splendid as long as we tell ourselves that what happened was our fault!

What happened was not our fault!

We didn't ask for it. We wore the shame; we took the blame. But it was not our fault! Those words are the only ones to tell yourself now, every day, if you are in the process of trying to heal, and that healing may take most of your life. But we are worth whatever amount of time it takes!

And above all, we must start talking about incest! We must COME OUT FROM UNDER and SPEAK OUT FROM UNDER Child Sexual Abuse. I have bared all in this book to show you one way to come out from under: writing your story. There are other ways and many victim/survivors are using them. They are writing books, blogs, poems and songs. They are painting pictures, sculpting, talking in groups and to groups. Spreading the word that ***we refuse to be silent any longer***!

Wonderful art is being born from pain. With every creation, the abused are becoming "more splendid", "more extraordinary", because that's what we are: we victims are extraordinary in what we have suffered and survived. Yes, many of us have been silent because we lacked the courage to speak up. We feared reprisal. But many of us have been silent because we cared more for someone else than for ourselves. I'd like to think that in being silent, we showed strength, not weakness. Unlike our abusers, we didn't put ourselves first! And in that respect, we are extraordinary in a world where it's always "me first!"

Your comments and reviews posted at GOODREADS and/or on my personal website at http://www.vigaboland.com
would be most appreciated. If you feel others could benefit from reading "NO TEARS FOR MY FATHER", please tell them about my book. Join me in my efforts to spread awareness of incest in families, to kill the denial that is re-victimizing victims day in and day out, and to encourage other victims to SPEAK OUT FROM UNDER INCEST and CHILD SEXUAL ABUSE.

Your friend in healing,
Viga Boland
www.vigaboland.com

COME OUT FROM UNDER POETRY

WHO AM I?

What you did to my body was bad
But what you did to my mind was worse
The body can heal itself
But the mind is forever cursed

Your belittling words demeaned
You called me name after name
You said I was something I wasn't
And I walked the halls of shame

Now your words still play in my head
Coloring every decision
I take two steps forward, one back
From any vision that isn't your vision

My body is slowly forgetting
But will my mind ever be free?
You turned me into something you wanted
But is that someone me?

Who am I?

©*Viga Boland*

COME OUT FROM UNDER POETRY

FOOTPRINTS

Our words are not footprints
Left along the shore
Waves will not erase them
They live forevermore

Tiny grains of sand
Ever shifting 'neath the tide
Bringing up the memories
Of pain so hard to hide

We must think before we speak
Choosing carefully what we say
So our words can open minds
And our footprints show the way

©*Viga Boland, 2012*

COME OUT FROM UNDER POETRY

You don't have to be strong all the time
Breaking down isn't a crime

It's not a crime to give 'em what for
To stamp your feet and slam the door

It isn't a crime if you want to yell
And tell the world to go to hell
None of that is a crime!
But it's a crime to bottle up
all the fear and pain inside
And it's a crime when you live in the shame
of secrets you try to hide

It wasn't you who wanted this
but it's you who's doing the time

So scream! Shout!
Let it all out!

YOU didn't commit the crime!

©*Viga Boland*

COME OUT FROM UNDER POETRY

Yes, you must face the pain
But reliving it again and again
Wallowing in despair gets you nowhere
except further under

You know you want to tell
You've tried for many years
You start to speak, then shut your mouth
And your face dissolves in tears
of fear and self-loathing

But this has to stop!
The abuser should feel the shame
The abuser should wear the guilt
The abuser is to blame
for what you feel

Reach out to those who care
Love yourself that much!
Let their open arms embrace you
And heal you with their touch

©*Viga Boland, 2012*

COME OUT FROM UNDER POETRY

We live in different worlds
Our paths are not the same
But together we've trudged long roads
paved with shame

We see each other in words
Each face is like our own
Bright smiles that hide the tears
That each of us has known

Like freshly fallen snow
Hides potholes hidden below
We trip and sometimes fall
but still pick ourselves up and go

Our battle has been tough
The journey has been long
But when we hold each other's hands
We make each other strong

The more we share our stories
The easier it is to tell
Come out from under with us
And let's close the gates on hell

©*Viga Boland, 2012*

COME OUT FROM UNDER POETRY

HANDS

They speak in private circles
And whisper 'mongst themselves
Of hands upon their bodies
When they were 3 or 6 or 12

Of hands meant to protect them
From monsters in the night
Of hands that touched a private place
And filled a child with fright

How sad the eyes of children
So wise beyond their years
When hands that stole their innocence
Didn't wipe away their tears

Nor cared how they were feeling
Nor tried to make things right
These hands belonged to monsters
Who took their lives at night

Now they speak in private circles
Setting masks aside
It's here that others understand
What monsters' hands denied

©*Viga Boland, 2012*

COME OUT FROM UNDER POETRY

If I could be a tree
I would be a willow
To weep my tears into a pond
Instead of on my pillow

Beneath my sweeping arms
I'd embrace the pain of others
The used, accused, belittled and used
My sisters and my brothers

Together we'd grow strong
Our tears would set us free
'Cause if I were that Willow
I'd weep no more for me

©*Viga Boland, 2012*

COME OUT FROM UNDER POETRY

Sometimes I think I suffered less than most
At the hands of that now, long dead ghost
Who trolls the halls of my subconscious mind
And picks at the scars that he left behind
Re-opening wounds I thought had healed
And disclosing secrets long concealed

But I no longer hurt like many of you
Nightmares and flashbacks are now so few
Perhaps it's because I'm so much older
Or simply that time has made me bolder
But the more I tell how he made me bleed
The less I hurt; the more I'm freed

My greatest wish for all of you
Is one day you'll feel as I do
That you'll realize the past is done
And put it away so you can move on
He won the battles but I won the war
That ghost can't hurt me anymore!

©*Viga Boland, 2012*

BLACK & BLUE

Music, Lyrics ©Andrew Rudd, Victoria Boland 2012

Do you hear the sound of the tear that's trickling down her face?
And can you see the stains that lie beneath her strained & tired eyes?

I do...and she is black & blue... She's black & blue

She hides it well beneath the mask she paints upon her shell but I can tell...
And even on a sunny day, her eyes reveal a sadder shade of grey...and they say

That it's true...
She is black & blue
She's black & blue

Pennies in a wishing well
She throws one in & says goodbye to this hell
She's been living in
Only she can change her life
Find the strength & love inside herself
To say....

That's she's through...with being black & blue
She's through...no more black & blue

She's through...with being black & blue
It's true...no more black & blue...no more black & blue
Do you hear the sound of the tear that's trickling down...

Watch a video put to this song at:
　http://www.youtube.com/watch?v=2mS97UgiwIw

DID YOU KNOW THIS ABOUT CHILD SEXUAL ABUSE IN CANADA?

1) Up to 90 % of people with addictions were sexually abused as children.

2) Up to 80% of inmates were sexually abused as children.

3) 49% of "homeless" women were sexually abused as children.

More Canadian Statistics

Just how big a problem IS this? How many children? Who does it affect? What is the impact to society?

Prevalence of Childhood Sexual Abuse:

-1 in 3 girls and 1 in 5 boys experience an unwanted sexual act before their 18th birthday.
-95 % of child sexual abuse victims know their perpetrator.
-30-40% of sexual assault victims are abused by a family member.
Non-parental relatives – 35% Friends and Peers – 15%
Stepfathers – 13%
Biological Fathers – 9% Other Acquaintances – 9%
Boyfriend/Girlfriend of Biological Parent – 5% Biological Mother – 5%
-Very few cases (2%) of substantiated sexual abuse involve a stranger.
-Child and youth victims who were sexually assaulted by family members were on average 9 years old compared to 12 years old for victims of non-family members.
-64% of sexual offences reported to police took place in a residence
-26% took place in public and open areas, and 11% took place in commercial places
-54% of girls and 31% of boys under 21 have experienced sexual abuse; (22% of female victims reported two or more sexual offences and 7% of male victims reported two or more sexual offences)
-In 2005, the rate of sexual assault against children and youth was over five times higher than for adults (206 children and youth victims compared to 39 adult victims for every 100,000 people.)

-Boys 4-7 years of age were 3 times more often the victims of sexual abuse than boys of other ages.
-Girls aged 4-7 and 12-17 were twice as likely to be victims of sexual abuse as girls aged 0-3 and 8-11.

Consequences of Childhood Sexual Abuse on the Individual

-70% of sexual abuse survivors report excessive use of drugs & alcohol.
-60% of women with panic disorder are victims of child sexual abuse.
-76% of prostitutes have a history of child sexual abuse.
-Child victims of sexual abuse have been found to display a wide range of symptomology, such as: low self-esteem, guilt, self blame, social withdrawal, marital and family problems, depression, somatic complaints, difficulties with sexuality, eroticized behavior and irrational fears.
-There has been retrospective correlation of psychiatric disorders in adulthood with unwanted childhood sexual experiences.
-The long-term consequences of childhood sexual experiences with adults have been demonstrated to include, anxiety, deliberate self-harm, depression, difficulties in interpersonal relationships, eating disorders, poor self-esteem, prostitution, and sexual dysfunction.
-Women who reported sexual abuse histories were more likely to report suicidal ideation at the time of hospitalization and a history of multiple suicide attempts.

* The information provided above is courtesy of the website, **VOICE FOUND**, *http://www.voicefound.ca*

Further information regarding the above is found at:

http://www.voicefound.ca/about/facts?goback= %2Egde_1867777_member_256033338

ABOUT THE AUTHOR

Viga Boland has been writing all her life: articles, poetry, editorials, book reviews, short stories, blog posts...whatever grabs her fancy. She has won awards for her poetry, had articles published in magazines in both Canada and Australia, and, as a fledgling author, was assigned the job of interviewing one of Canada's greatest female authors back in the 70's: **Margaret Laurence**. You can read Viga's interview with Margaret on her website at http://www.vigaboland.com

But it wasn't until her retirement that Viga finally found enough time to write a book. She didn't expect her first book would be a memoir, but after revealing a secret hidden for over 40 years, she had to agree with her family that her true story of incest needed to be told. Her first memoir, **"No Tears for my Father"** earned her Gold Medal in the Readers Favorite 2104 Book Awards. Her follow-up memoir, written at the request of fans, **"Learning to Love Myself"** tells the story of her recovery and self-discovery through the love of her husband and children. *Read Chapter 1 of that book on the next page.* Her 3rd and probably last memoir, **"The Ladies of Loretto"** is a complete departure from the style and content of the first two memoirs. It's a tongue-in-cheek, funny recollection of her 4 years as a student in a Catholic High School for Girls in the 1960's. If you love to laugh, don't miss this book.

All Viga's books are available in both softcover and digital format for all e-readers, including Kindle, directly from her author's website store: www.vigaboland.com/store Viga's latest passion is editing & publishing a magazine for memoir writers, "Memoirabilia". Learn more at http://www.memoirabilia.ca

LEARNING TO LOVE MYSELF

A Memoir of recovery after abuse and self-discovery of someone worthy of her own love and that of others. Available in both softcover and digital format for all e-readers directly from the author's website: www.vigaboland.com

Chapter 2: The Honeymoon

"So, how do you like the idea of roughing it?"
"I don't...much..."
We were discussing honeymoon plans over breakfast at our tiny cluttered table/desk. As teachers, we had the long summer break ahead of us.
"But it'll be fun," John persisted. His eyes twinkled with excitement at the possibilities of seeing places never yet seen. "We have time to travel Canada as far East as Newfoundland. By camping, we can afford to do what neither of us has ever done: see a good deal of this country. Quebec has such wonderful old architecture. We can visit Ottawa and see the parliament buildings. Then we head for the Atlantic provinces...all the way to the rugged coastline, maybe even into the US for a bit at Maine. It'll be amazing. And all the photos I can take! What do you think?"
I didn't think much of the idea at all. It was hardly the honeymoon I had in mind. I would have preferred what Rico (whose heart I'd broken) had suggested to me years ago: a honeymoon in Italy, gliding in a gondola in Venice, throwing coins into the Trevi Fountain...so much more romantic than camping in a pup tent in mosquito-infested woods and bathing in cold Canadian lakes. Nothing romantic about driving thousands of miles day after day, pitching a tent, and cooking canned beans over a campfire.
"But it'll be fun!" John persisted. "A lot more fun than flying to one location, staying in fancy, over-priced hotels, paying a fortune for every meal, and only seeing one place instead of hundreds. What don't you like about it? Let's face it: we don't have much money. If we run out, we can turn around and head home. I'm just being practical..."
Yes, there it was. If John was anything, as I was

learning quickly, he was practical. Even well before the wedding, on my birthday, he'd given me a gift in a huge box. Excited, I'd opened it to find a large wall clock. I was speechless. A wall clock? As nice as its diamond-shaped brown and gold frame was, what kind of birthday gift was that for a guy to give his girlfriend of a few months?

"I'm just being practical," he'd said. "I figured since we were going to get married one day, this would be more useful than some silly, little meaningless gift. Don't you agree this makes more sense?"

I looked at his handsome face and sensed his delight in giving me such a practical gift, but in my insecurity and shock, I'd merely mumbled, "It's very...er...nice. Thanks."

And as much as he was practical, he was also frugal, very frugal. His practical frugality caused one of our first disagreements right after we finally vacated the bed the day after the wedding to do a badly needed grocery shopping. As we pushed the buggy down the dairy aisle of the local supermarket, he'd reached for a tub of the cheapest margarine on the shelf at the same time that I grabbed a pound of the delicious, but expensive Lactantia butter.

"We don't need that, do we?" He asked in surprise, eyeing the butter in my hand. "It's so expensive!"

"But I've never eaten margarine!" I countered. The very idea disgusted me. My mother only ever used butter. "That margarine you're holding is horrible stuff."

"What's wrong with it?" John looked indignant, even slightly offended. "My mother used margarine all the time. All three kids were raised on it and we're all healthy. And it costs one hell of a lot less than butter! It's just good sense to use something more economical to do the same thing, isn't it? I'm just being practical, love."

Reluctantly, even somewhat resentful, I put the Lactantia back on the shelf. So this was how it was going to be, I thought to myself. I'd just left a home where a man had ruled my every thought, action and decision for nearly twenty-four years. Was another man now going to tell me what to do for the rest of my life?

I fought the tiny wave of anger niggling at me. I wanted that butter! I'd gag eating margarine! John sensed my hesitation and smiled at me. I wanted to stay mad but I couldn't. Oh what the heck! It was only a little thing, and yes, I suppose it made sense to save pennies where we could. Since my father had insisted I don't touch the vacation pay they needed for the upcoming mortgage payment, we only had John's pay on which to live. Margarine made sense.

So did a camping honeymoon I decided as I got up to clear the breakfast dishes off the table.

"Okay," I agreed with as much enthusiasm as I could muster. "Camping it is!"

NO TEARS FOR MY FATHER: PART II

Learning To Love Myself

A memoir of healing after child sexual abuse

Viga Boland

On the next page...an excerpt from "The Ladies of Loretto" available in both softcover and digital formats for all readers from www.vigaboland.com

***Below: An EXCERPT from Viga Boland's 3rd memoir,
"THE LADIES OF LORETTO"***

*Available only from the author's website at
<u>www.vigaboland.com/store</u>*

At the dance, the nuns are everywhere. I think the entire convent is on patrol watching for any unladylike behaviour. I stand at the side of the gym, watching the couples dancing and wishing I had a date. Here I am, not that far off 18, and not allowed to date.

Betty and her beau move discreetly to the music. There's Gerry, super tall now, with an even taller partner. I return her smirk when she catches me looking at them and I shrink further back into the darkness along the walls.

"Would you like to dance?" asks a swarthy, but rather handsome guy with a dark complexion.

I look to each side of me thinking he must be addressing someone else, but he reaches for my hand and pulls me onto the floor. I shut out the image of my father's face that intrudes onto the moment. This is it. I'm nervous as the boy puts his arm around my waist and pulls me close against him. I feel a rush. His masculinity is pressing hard on my privates. Yikes! But suddenly, something else is pressed hard between us forcing us apart: it's a 12-inch ruler held by one of the nuns.

"Too close!" she admonishes. "Your bodies are too close. They must not be touching. They should be 12-inches apart."

She holds the ruler there till my partner loosens his grip on my waist and pulls his body away. We continue to dance but the thrill is gone. He doesn't ask me for a second dance. I'm not surprised. I kept stepping on his feet. I resume my spot in the shadows along the wall, watching Miriam and wondering if she and her boyfriend do more than just dance closely.

About a week later, I find the answer to my musings about Miriam. She comes to me looking embarrassed and scared.

"Heidi, I think I might be pregnant," she whispers.

FROM OUR FAMILY TO YOURS

WE WISH YOU LOVE

www.vigaboland.com
www.memoirabilia.ca

Printed in Great Britain
by Amazon